Simplicity, Intricacy, and Beyond:

Science, Religion, Politics, and Cards, Hypervolume III

Simplicity, Intricacy, and Beyond: Science, Religion, Politics, and Cards, Hypervolume III

Maurice James Blair

Synapsid Revelations Press

Simplicity, Intricacy, and Beyond: Science, Religion, Politics, and Cards, Hypervolume III

ISBN: 978-1-963470-13-0

© Copyright 2024 by Maurice James Blair. All Rights Reserved. No portion of this may be copied in any manner, except for as provided by the fair use of copyrighted materials and/or if properly arranged such as to receive advanced written permission from the author and/or the publisher.

The information herein is accurate to the best of the knowledge of the author and the publisher as of the time of going to print.

Blair, Maurice James

Synapsid Revelations Press Corporation
9619 Meadowcroft Dr
Houston, TX 77063

1. Social Psychology 2. Memoir 3. History
4. Comparative Religion 5. Health and Wellness
6. Politics 7. Art I. Title

The main composition spanned from Various Dates of August 2024 to The First Ten Days of September 2024. Publication Date: September 11, 2024: Patriot Day

After 11 SEP database transmission constituted an act of publishing, minimal text changes happened 13-14 SEP 2024.

PREFACE

Considering random statements out of context in the first six chapters would in many cases be like witnessing a headline.

Such could otherwise appear via any of many different books, articles, and websites. However, the author and the publisher have taken efforts for the overall pattern to be insightful, whether or not a given observer judges its mix of omissions, transmissions, and interpretations to be jumbled, unjumbled, banal, elite, orderly, garish, lavish, or anything else.

In most cases, a given statement in isolation is easily corroborated by any of a multitude of easily accessible sources. Therefore, there are few attributions of specific sources. Where there are such attributions, their inclusion likely facilitates enhanced understanding and/or a smoother fact checking process for those choosing such a pursuit. There is also some original content.

That being said, the triangulations, quadrangulations, and other coordinative processes of developing this work included consultations with: *Webster's Encyclopedic Unabridged Dictionary of the English Language* (1989), *The Timetables of History: A Horizontal Linkage of People and Events* (Grun, Bernard, 1901-1972; Simon & Schuster; 1979 updated version), *The Adi-Buddha* (Hazra, Kanai Lal, 1986, reprinted 2018), events, Wikipedia entries, Conservapedia entries, music, television, driving, radio, phone calls, zazen, stretching, resistance training, and going for walks.

Graphics and extended narratives are all attributable to the author unless stated otherwise or otherwise easily inferred. Graphics, artwork, diagrams, narratives, photographs, hybrids, etc.

To reiterate something expressed early in *Science, Religion, Politics, and Cards*, though with multiple subtle adjustments and major simplification:

The author and the publisher avoided any intentional duplication of exact expressions from others except for: 1) cases of giving full credit to the others, 2) cases in which de minimis amounts of patterns render them freely usable when fitting adjacent surroundings in such manners as to sufficiently differentiate from the source items, and 3) de minimis use of public domain materials.

Simplicity, Intricacy, and Beyond:

Science, Religion, Politics, and Cards
Hypervolume III

(The cover design and this variation of it are by a collaboration between Paramita Bhattacharjee {of Creative Paramita} and Maurice James Blair {of Synapsid Revelations Press}.)

Table of Contents

PREFACE iii

INTRODUCTION: SELECT ARTWORK, PHOTOGRAPHY, AND HYBRIDS 1

CHAPTER ONE: 1790-1900 9

CHAPTER TWO: 1901-2000 11

CHAPTER THREE: VARIOUS GLIMPSES OF THE JANUARY 2001 TO JUNE 2024 PERIOD 17

CHAPTER FOUR: A COPY OF PAGES 3-8 OF A PREVIOUSLY PUBLISHED OPEN LETTER TO THE FBI, FOLLOWED BY A FEW ADDITIONAL COMMENTS 21

CHAPTER FIVE: JULY 2024 31

CHAPTER SIX: AUGUST 2024 33

CHAPTER SEVEN: A FEW GLIMPSES OF SEPTEMBER 2024 AND GATEWAYS INTO EVERYTHING ELSE 35

CHAPTER EIGHT: MORE SETS OF PHOTOS & ARTISTIC DESIGNS & NARRATIVES 50

ENDNOTES 129

EPILOGUE: A PROJECTION FOR THE PERIOD FROM DECEMBER 31, 2024 TO A WHILE ONWARD 133

INTRODUCTION: SELECT ARTWORK, PHOTOGRAPHY, AND HYBRIDS

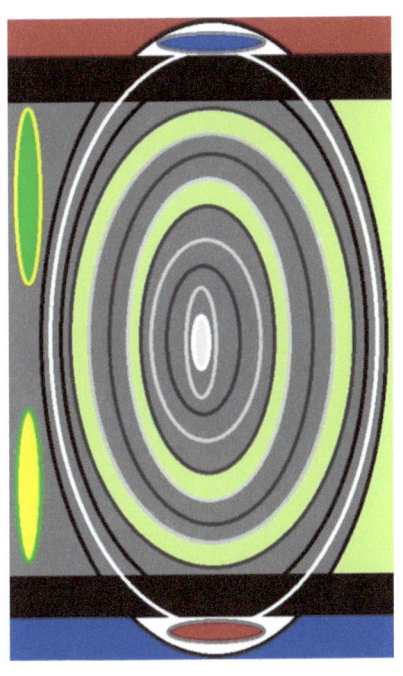

A January 21, 2022 View of Gary, Indiana

"Untitled 2021 MarCh"

"2112 Multiverse BA Alpha Gate"

"2023_5_25_0651modifiedArtwork0716"

INTRODUCTION

"PLPLKSW 20210728"

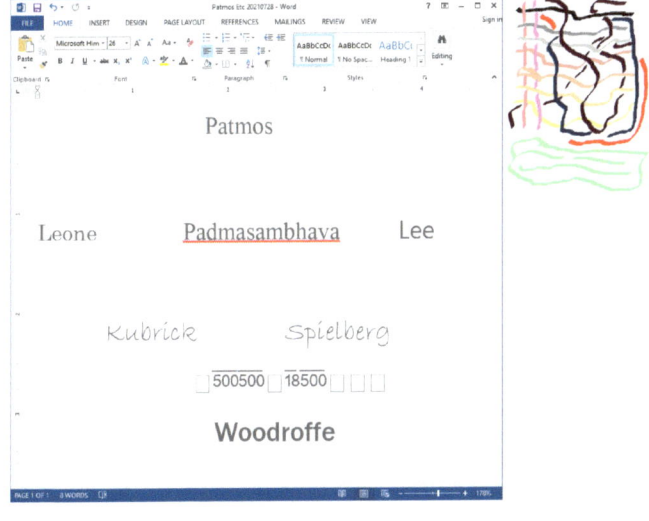

"Digital Nondigital"

"Take 3 of Possible FC for ES ATUAO"

8   Simplicity, Intricacy, and Beyond: S.R.P.C., Hypervol. III

"Digital Nondigital II"

Digital Nondigital II

Existence   Nonexistence
           Arts   Nonarts
        Mysteries   Nonmysteries
     Natures   Exordium Terminus   Nonnatures
   Sciences   Nonsciences
                 Transcendental
  Religions   Nonreligions
        Binary   Nonbinary   Binary
 Unions Exordium Terminus αΩ Exordium Terminus Nonunions
        Nontranscendental Transcendental Nontranscendental
  Sports   Nonsports
                 Nonbinary
    Courts   Noncourts
        Philosophies Exordium Terminus Nonphilosophies
           Games   Nongames
              Fullness   Emptiness
 Nonexistence   Existence

   Nonreligions Noncourts Emptiness   Fullness Courts Religions
   Nonunions Nonsports Nonmysteries Mysteries Sports Unions

CHAPTER ONE: 1790-1900

January 1, 1790: Some of the people observing the Gregorian Calendar greet its 1790.

January 8, 1790: United States President Washington delivers the first State of the Union Address of the United States of America.

January 14, 1790: Alexander Hamilton proposes a payment plan for U.S. debt. The ensuing process of debate and approval serves to warn about the related dangers emerging from national debt.

April 17, 1790: Benjamin Franklin dies, after having been born in 1706, helped with much science, diplomacy, political revolution, and practical wisdom.

May 31, 1790: The U.S. enacts its first copyright act. Technically: Act of May 31, 1790, ch. 15, § 1, 1 Stat. 124 (1790 Act). Informally: The 1790 Copyright Act.

July 17, 1790: Scottish political economist Adam Smith dies, after having been born in 1723 and clarified and expounded on a great many models and principles of human interaction.

December 31, 1790: Some observe New Year's Eve.

January 1, 1791: Some observe New Year's Day.

1791: U.S. Treasury Secretary Alexander Hamilton founds The Federalist Party.

1792: U.S. Secretary of State Thomas Jefferson founds The Democratic-Republican Party.

January 21, 1793: Charles-Henri Sanson executes King Louis XVI of France. The latter had been born in 1754 into royalty and had subsequently struggled with multiple controversial and challenging situations.

May 27, 1793: Elizabeth "Eliza" Pinckney dies after having a) been born in 1722 as Elizabeth Lucas, b) married Charles Pinckney (1699-1758), c) become a widow upon his death, and d) popularized the use of indigo as a cash crop

June 20-22, 1793: Within the Haitian Revolution occurs the Battle of Cap-Français.

September 28, 1793: Rani Rashmoni was born in the Bengal Presidency within British India.

July 4, 1804: Charles-Henri Sanson dies, after having been born in 1739 and having served as a professional executioner in the process of delivering capital punishment to over 2,900 individual human beings.

February 19, 1861: Rani Rashmoni dies, after having served as a businesswoman and a leading activist.

January 1, 1863: U.S. President Abraham Lincoln issues an executive order that would be officially known as Proclamation 95 and informally known as The Emancipation Proclamation.

It serves as part of a multimillenial process of the rising, falling, and rising again of the works fostering and improving human liberty.

December 31, 1900: Many observe a New Year's Eve.

CHAPTER TWO: 1901-2000

January 1, 1901: Many observe a New Year's Day. An official process establishes the nation frequently known as Australia, more formally known as The Commonwealth of Australia, as its founders arrange for its legal independence.

February 27, 1901: The Sultan of Turkey orders troops to the Bulgarian frontier.

November 11, 1918: Armistice Day marks the End of The Great War (which had started in 1914).

1922: *Nosferatu: A Symphony of Horror* reaches movie audiences. A series that shows a copy of samples of its imagery spans portions of this page and the next:

Glimpses of F.W. Murnau's *Nosferatu*, cont'd:

CHAPTER TWO

1934: *Of Human Bondage* arrives into movie theaters, entertaining and enlightening many beings. Two glimpses of a character portrayed by Bette Davis:

1938: Scientists, who had previously believed the Coelacanth to have been extinct for many millions of years, discover the species to be alive and well.

1939-1945: World War II happens: People choose to refer to "The Great War" as having been "World War One." The psychological and sociological bondages enslaving humans from within their psyches cause "The Second Great War" to be, as judged by many, much more horrific than virtually anything previously witnessed on Earth. Near the end of "WW2," the United States ushers in the age of nuclear weapons by using two of them to devastate Japan.

Some consider it a win for the Allies, others consider it a win for no one.

1944-2000: Technology booms. Advances in medicine, transportation, the study of outer space, meteorology, computer science, mathematics, physics, engineering, and other fields move at frenetic paces.

1945-2000: Human transformations and meditations continue. Within the period of what some consider the last five-and-a-half decades of the third millennium, many contemplate questions such as:

• "Was the Holocaust that happened in connection with World War Two more of a Jewish tragedy, more a combination of a Roma tragedy and a Jewish tragedy, or more of a Human tragedy? If substantially a hybrid of all three, then how much?"

• "How much awareness do various classes of beings other than humans possess?"

• "How central or peripheral is The Human Race to The Totality of Reality?"

• "How do Minds relate to The Rest of Reality?"

• "To what degree is Cultural Relativism correct?"

• "To what degree is Cultural Absolutism correct?"

• "How vital is Liberty, and how should we best negotiate situations in which more Liberty for each of multiple competitors involves a tradeoff with each of the other competitors?"

CHAPTER TWO

1947: Executioners hang Former Slovakian President Jozef Tiso (who had been born in 1887) to death. The New York Yankees win the MLB World Series. British driver John Cobb sets a new world land speed record of 394.196 miles per hour.

1949: Arthur Miller's stage play *Death of a Salesman* premieres. The U.S.S.R. tests its first nuclear bomb. Composer Richard Strauss (who had been born in 1864) dies. Philip Hench discovers cortisone. The Richard Rodgers and Oscar Hammerstein II musical *South Pacific* premiers.

1968: The Rolling Stones music album *Beggars Banquet* becomes available for sale. A controversial edition of The Summer Olympics happens and spurs people to think more thoroughly about issues of social justice, equity, equality, liberty, socioeconomic differences, etc.

June 15, 1970: Charles Manson goes on trial for a set of murders involving actions by his cult.

1970: The first observation of Earth Day occurs. The music album *Led Zeppelin III* reaches publication.

June 15, 1972: A bomb destroys Cathay Pacific Flight 700Z over a portion of Southeast Asia.

October 5, 1987: The music album *Heaven on Earth* by Belinda Carlisle reaches publication.

October 14-19, 1987: The DJIA drops precipitously.

May 17, 1989: Approximately one million protestors march through Beijing in support for human rights.

June 4, 1989: The Tiananmen Square Incident happens in Beijing, China, resulting in the deaths of many protestors—the deaths of many dedicated human rights supporters.

October 6, 1989: His Holiness The 14th Dalai Lama wins the Nobel Peace Prize.

October 9, 1989 happens.

December 10, 1989 happens.

1990: The San Francisco 49ers win Super Bowl XXIV. The Detroit Pistons win the NBA Finals. Germany reunifies. A magnitude-7.7 earthquake hits Luzon, an island in the Philippines.

June 12-15, 1991: Mount Pinatubo erupts.

June 15, 1991: Mount Pinatubo explodes, sending an ash cloud 25 miles into the atmosphere.

November 23, 2000: Several *Financial Times* headlines and bylines:

- "Bush attacks Florida judgment" by Edward Alden in Washington and Richard Wolffe in Austin, Texas

- "Mexican cabinet faces reform battle" by Henry Tricks and Andrea Mandel Campbell in Mexico City

- "Flurry of opposition stalls EU postal liberalisation plans" by Deborah Hargreaves

CHAPTER THREE: VARIOUS GLIMPSES OF THE JANUARY 2001 TO JUNE 2024 PERIOD

January 20, 2001: The inauguration of U.S. President George W. Bush combines with the departure of U.S. President Bill Clinton from the American presidency.

March 18, 2002: The United States of America invades Afghanistan as a follow-up to what had happened on September 11, 2001.

2004: Greece hosts the Summer Olympics, yet its economic situation encounters much extra difficulty.

2008-2009: Many raise concerns about what they believe to be dangers for if Barrack Obama would win the U.S. Presidency, and he wins the general election anyway. President Obama, other world leaders, and business leaders negotiate with each other economic realities as they navigate a Global Financial Crisis.

2009-2016: President Obama and other American leaders deal with many issues of racial tension within the United States and several tensions between the vying factions of an array of nation-states.

2016-2017: Many raise concerns about what they believe to be dangers for if Donald Trump would win the U.S. Presidency. Amid hyperpolarization, he wins the general election anyway.

2019-2020: Jordan Peele hosts a manifestation of *The Twilight Zone*.

January 2021: Both in the U.S.A. and abroad, many Americans become super-worried about the U.S.

February 7, 2021: The Tampa Bay Buccaneers win Super Bowl LV.

August 30, 2021: The United States of America completes its withdrawal from Afghanistan, in what some deem a carryover effect from a combination of 1998, 2001, 2002, 2012, 2016, 2020, 1492-1990, etc.

July 31, 2022: In Nevada, a man says out loud in public at Harry Reid International Airport that in the brief period after the August 6, 1945 nuclear bombing of Hiroshima and before the August 15 (as by some time zones) / August 14 (as by others) Japanese surrender such as to end WW2 in most regular senses, he and other U.S. military service members flew on multiple airplane missions over Japan in order to make Japanese wonder if another atom bomb would soon drop.

Although there was one more such atomic detonation during that period, specifically on August 9, 1945 at Nagasaki, the idea of the extra flights was to psychologically intimidate.[1]

November 5, 2022: The Houston Astros complete their victory of the 2022 MLB World Series.

November 1, 2023: The Texas Rangers complete their victory of the 2023 MLB World Series.

January 28, 2024: The Kansas City Chiefs win the AFC Championship Game. The San Francisco 49ers win the NFC Championship Game.

February 11, 2024: The Kansas City Chiefs win Super Bowl LVIII.

May 30, 2024: A New York jury convicts President Donald Trump of multiple felonies. Many Trump supporters continue to support him. Many Trump critics continue to vilify him. The most intense of his supporters consider him the main hope for the future of the country. The most intense of his critics consider him the biggest threat to the future of the country. Others do not know what to make of all of this with his attempt to win back the presidency.

June 2024: Tensions between China and its neighbors continue. Some include conflict between the P.R.O.C. and the R.O.C. as among those. Tensions between disparate Middle Eastern factions continue. The Russia-Ukraine War continues. Extreme rhetoric continues back and forth between those affiliated with different political parties worldwide. Poverty in parts of Africa, Asia, Europe, Australia, South America, and North America continues. Nonprofit organization, business, and governmental operations continue nearly worldwide. Some continue considering the concept of separateness-versus-unity to be intricate.

June 2024, cont'd:

• Republican pundits continue alleging the Democratic Party to threaten the future of liberty and human rights both in the United States and elsewhere.

• Democratic pundits continue alleging the Republican Party to threaten the future of liberty and human rights both in the United States and elsewhere.

• Calls for President Joe Biden to relinquish his bid for reelection escalate.

• Independent voters continue to repeatedly shift in percentages of support for the Democrats and support for the Republicans according to the polls.

• News reports of scientific advances continue.

• Births, deaths, and marriages continue.

• Much else continues on the planet that some call Terra and others call Earth, and which at least a few go back and forth between calling Terra and calling Earth.

CHAPTER FOUR: A COPY OF PAGES 3-8 OF A PREVIOUSLY PUBLISHED OPEN LETTER TO THE FBI, FOLLOWED BY A FEW ADDITIONAL COMMENTS

A.O.L.T.F.B.I.O.116A.T.T.E.&T.D.A.T.A.

From: Maurice James Blair
To: The United States Federal Bureau of Investigation
Cc: Anyone Else Who Might Ever Encounter This Work
Transmission Date: July 01, 2024 (i.e., The Day After)

Dear FBI Agent(s) and/or Other FBI Personnel,

Recently, I arranged for multiple copies of *Alternative Beginnings and Endings of All Things: Science, Religion, Politics, and Cards, Hypervolume II* to go to your main office. I trust that you have received at least one such copy.

As you are likely aware of, early in that book there is a mention that my publisher and I planned on sending at least one copy to you, and that my publisher and I were fully committed to attempt absolute honesty in the process of composing that work. Having identified a few anomalies in the text, this letter shall identify relevant instances best to bring to your attention. It shall then present a supplemental timeline and commentary.

The copies sent to you were of the regular distribution hardcover, which received revision on May 24, 2024 to cut down on typos and other anomalies from what the promotional paperback had in it. Both the revised on 5/23/2024 promotional paperback and the revised on 5/24/2024 regular distribution hardcover corrected for one weird digit reversal that the 5/21/2024 publication date transmission into the aggregator database somehow included. Declining refinement beyond the 5/23 to 5/24/2024 processing allowed its text finalization to precede several high-profile events that happened in its wake and allowed the possibility of this follow-up letter.

CHAPTER FOUR

Here are items subsequently noticed and best to receive acknowledgment in this letter:

- The reference to December 5, 2014 on page 56 involved some of what happened on December 12, 2014. Therefore, a standardized version of the sentence with that would be, "On December 12, 2014, he and I played two chess games (i.e., one each way for color coordination), and I won both games in convincing fashion."
- The spelling McEntyre on page 693 was in connection with the name McEntire. It appears that a subconscious deflection from McEntire into the direction of MacIntyre resulted in the spelling McEntyre.
- On page 313 there appeared the spelling John where in that context rendering the standard spelling would have appeared as Jon.
- The song title reference on page 609 shown as "The Place Where Time Stands Still" would have been more standard in its context if it had shown as "Where Time Stands Still."
- Solvable omissions, in which omitted words or phrases can be ascertained by an astute reader without being told what they are. Examples: • stating "circa February" where all the rest of the context made it clear that "circa December" within the same calendar year was the intended reference; "circa ten months after Febraury" • a solvable omission of "Enforcement to Forensics Six" • a solvable omission of "Two, Structure to Ethical Economics" or "Ethical Economics Two, Structure to" • a case of spelling "to" backwards

A.O.L.T.F.B.I.O.116A.T.T.E.&T.D.A.T.A.

Synapsid Revelations Press Corporation is considering the option of including a copy of the main text of pages 3-8 of this letter, and/or excerpts thereof, in at least one subsequent work.

The main delivery method of this will probably involve posting a link to the web page for the ebooklet via X (formerly known as Twitter).

A timeline and supplemental commentary:

- 1986: The space shuttle Challenger exploded with a crew on board. The Chernobyl nuclear reactor exploded. The U.S. changed its policies in multiple ways that would prove controversial.

- 1993: The (Branch Davidian vs. FBI) Waco Siege occurred, and it involved much controversy. Vince Foster (1945-1993) died in circumstances that some would soon consider highly suspicious.

- April 19, 1995: The Oklahoma City Bombing happened. Timothy James McVeigh (1968-2001) would subsequently claim that his outrage over the 1993 Waco Siege was a huge part of what motivated him to perpetrate that.

- June 16, 2015: Real Estate Mogul Donald Trump announced that he would run for U.S. President. Immigration reform was one of the topics that he emphasized in his speech.

CHAPTER FOUR

A.O.L.T.F.B.I.O.116A.T.T.E.&T.D.A.T.A.

- September 9, 2015: A news article mentioned that a 1927 news report had named Fred Trump (1905-1999) as having been arrested at a KKK parade. The patterns brought clouds of suspicion into the minds of many, who could ponder such scenarios as: #S1: Donald Trump's father, Fred Trump, was a member of the Ku Klux Klan. Scenario #S2: Donald Trump's father, Fred Trump, was never a member of the Ku Klux Klan. #S3: A multiple-universe set includes at least one universe in which scenario #S1 is accurate, and at least one universe in which the scenario #S2 is accurate.
(Cf. https://boingboing.net/2015/09/09/1927-news-report-donald-trump.html)
- October 2015 to June 2024: There occurred a pattern in which many conservatives believed that the FBI, the CIA, and other federal agencies have exhibited extreme liberal bias, which some have characterized as involving "a two-tiered justice system," whereas many liberals have believed that the FBI, the CIA, and other federal agencies have exhibited reasonable fairness.
- Consider variations of how to compare and contrast, for example, the federal government's treatment during that period of President Obama, President Trump, The Trump Family, National Security Advisor Flynn, President Clinton, Secretary of State Clinton, President Biden, The Biden Family, etc.
(Cf. *both* Wikipedia.org & Conservapedia.com.)

A.O.L.T.F.B.I.O.116A.T.T.E.&T.D.A.T.A.

- There could be multitudes of theories that sentient beings could have about how much relationship each item in this timeline has with each of the other items in this timeline.

- I honestly do not know much of *what gives* about this entire set of controversies. In contrast, I believe that the process that led to the writing and publication of *Alternative Beginnings and Endings of All Things* (2024) arrived at a medium-to-high degree of genuine understanding of some of the most vital elements of *what gives* about this entire set of controversies, as well as many of the other controversies of our reality.

- Although you, the personnel of the FBI, in many cases know a moderately-high amount of both public and nonpublic information about this set of controversies, here is a reminder that a significant percentage of the American populace—perhaps often ranging from about 35% to about 65% at any given instant—has been and is rather skeptical about how much, if any, you genuinely know and understand about *what gives* about all of this.

CHAPTER FOUR

A.O.L.T.F.B.I.O.116A.T.T.E.&T.D.A.T.A.

In lieu of providing a handwritten signature, I am coordinating with others to have an online ebooklet of this work available for virtually anyone with Internet access to be able to encounter and to coordinate to post a link to this via X (formerly known as Twitter) as Maurice Blair (@M_James_Blair), such as to alert you, the FBI, and others about its existence and availability.

Also, a few print copies will probably go into circulation.

An Alternative Explanation of the Timing of This:
Main Composition Date: June 30, 2024
Revision, Expansion, and Editing Date: July 01, 2024

Another Explanation of the Timing of This: Somewhat Earlier than Midway Through the Year 2151 As Measured by Any of Several Variations of The Tibetan Calendar. Though At Least a Few Other Variations of The Tibetan Calendar Would Characterize It as Being Somewhat Earlier than Midway Through the Year 1770

Please note that in early July I included @FBI in an X post to publicly inform them and the general public of the https://mixam.com/share/6682b4c207ba1e6c4f7d965f URL free ebook of it. Also that month, I attempted to send three print copies to the Atlanta FBI office via a package, yet USPS tracking took a weird turn soon after that.

On another note, the way things have eventually gone, although I feel great about life and although I picked up a few followers on the X platform from June 4, 2024 onward, I still recognize every so often in a variety of ways that whatever value I might have to the human race at this stage of my life going forward, as of portions of the third quarter of 2024, that is, it sure seems to me that it is probably only of a moderate amount of value in many respects.

There have been several times in 3Q 2024 that I have actively thought toward THE LORD that it might be best for everyone involved if someone who would deserve the death penalty might murder me, get caught, get convicted, become sentenced to be executed, then get executed, and that if that would be for the very best for the future of whatever is true about religion and spirituality, then I would like to invite THE LORD to consider going for it in terms of influencing things to go that direction, because I feel great about how my life has gone yet at times seriously question what value I may offer to REALITY while maintaining the living biological form going forward at this stage.

In contrast, there have also been several times in 3Q 2024 that I have very much felt enthusiasm for the possibility of new rounds of experiencing varieties of including possession of a living, biological human body at this stage. Whichever way this goes, including to whatever degree any sort of identity and/or existence involves THE LORD, amid all the religious, scientific, and philosophical debates, I continue to be thankful

CHAPTER FOUR 29

for life, thankful for reality, and, to at least some degree, thankful for the way we have to deal with such a mixture of the known and the unknown.

RETURN ATTENTION NOW TO THE ISSUE OF A FEW MORE TECHNICAL CORRECTIONS &/OR STANDARDIZATIONS REGARDING ANOMALOUS ITEMS WITHIN THE PREVIOUS HYPERVOLUME OF THIS SERIES.

Although Chapter 10, Section 5, Part Q of *Alternative Beginnings and Endings of All Things* (2024) by Maurice James Blair has a sentence that includes "by Mark R. Levin" while a few phrases later omitting "by David Corn" within the same sentence, it should be obvious to most observers that that omitted phrase was part of the intended reference.

Also, bear in mind that the way the name "Joachim" appeared on page 384 was actually in reference to the name "Joaquin." Minds can sometimes conflate the actor Joaquin Pheonix with at least one Joachim man.

Filling in two spots of Ch. 7, Pt. 3 of ABAEOAT renders those more complete as: • "3. Enforcement to Forensics Three. Enforcement to Chemistry Six." • "6. Subjective to Ethical Economics Two. Structure to Ethical Economics Five."

On another note, the set from page 349 to page 358 (to comprise an article copy) actually omitted a small part of that article, a portion that otherwise would have appeared between what became page 357 and what became page 358. The omission is a combination of the title to a part and the first paragraph of that part.

The Other Portion of the Section 5 of the 4:18 P.M. U.S. Central Daylight Time Display of the article "Perhaps the Dawning of a New Tarot Deck"
(previously omitted b/w page three hundred fifty-seven & page three hundred fifty-eight of A.B.A.E.O.A.T.)

Part Four: Second Alternate Version

Because P.D. Ouspensky's 1913 essay "The Symbolism of the Tarot" included both the Rider-Waite VIII/XI inversion and an additional inversion of V & VII, there can be another alternate version of the deck proposed in this article: the same as the main alternate version just outlined, except with "V. Competition" and "VII. Business Philosophy."

CHAPTER FIVE: JULY 2024

July 4, 2024: Americans celebrate the 248th anniversary of the adoption of the United States Declaration of Independence.

July 13, 2024: A bullet strikes the right ear of President Donald Trump, yet he survived with only a modest amount of physical harm. The would-be assassin, Thomas Matthew Crooks (who was born in 2003), shoots from a distance, then dies immediately as the Secret Service Counter Sniper Team in defense of both President Trump and those nearby shoots that sniper-and-would-be-assassin dead. President Trump stays down briefly, then stands back up, then raises a fist to the air and yells, "Fight! Fight! Fight!"

July 14, 2024: President Joe Biden speaks to the general public in a manner of encouraging people to respect public officials and their families sufficiently such as to refrain from targeting them for assassination attempts, physical assault, etc.

July 15 to July 18, 2024: The 2024 Republican National Convention happens.

July 21, 2024: President Joe Biden's bid for reelection ends via a written statement in which, in addition to withdrawing that bid, he indicates a preference for Kamala Harris to become the Democratic Party's new nominee.

****

July 31, 2024: A sudden explosion kills Hamas Chairman Ismail Haniyeh (who was born about 5/8 of the way into the 20th century A.D./C.E., which was a little more than six decades prior).

July 1-31, 2024: Tensions between Israeli Prime Minister Benjamin Netanyahu, other Israelis, and people from other Middle Eastern nations rise and fall repeatedly.

****

CHAPTER SIX: AUGUST 2024

August 1-31, 2024: Political debates between people of various political, religious, scientific, and regional affiliations continue.

August 19 to August 22, 2024: The 2024 Democratic National Convention happens.

August 29, 2024: The U.S. national debt reached $35,279,776,145,434.29, including debt held by the public in the amount of $28,132,284,797,344.23. The remainder consisted of intergovernmental holdings.[2]

August 29, 2024: The Telegraph publishes a story titled, "Nasa makes discovery 'as important as gravity' about Earth."
Cf. that as accessible as of August 30, 2024 at URLs:
• https://www.telegraph.co.uk/news/2024/08/29/nasa-discovers-electric-field-surrounding-earth/
• https://www.msn.com/en-us/news/technology/nasa-makes-discovery-as-important-as-gravity-about-earth/ar-AA1pEuva

The Midnight Between August 2024 and September 2024 Marks What Some Consider Part of That September Without Being Part of That August, Whereas It Also Marks What Others Consider To Transcend All Mixtures of Being Part of Both of Those Months and Not Being Part of Both of Those Months.[3]

34 Simplicity, Intricacy, and Beyond: S.R.P.C., Hypervol. III

CHAPTER SEVEN: A FEW GLIMPSES OF SEPTEMBER 2024 AND GATEWAYS INTO EVERYTHING ELSE

Picchi, Aimee. "Thousands of hotel workers are on strike. Here's a list of hotels that are impacted." September 2, 2204. CBS News.
https://www.cbsnews.com/news/hotel-strike-boston-seattle-hawaii-marriott-hyatt-which-hotels-impacted/

Blair, Maurice. "Tackling Several Pressing Criminal Justice and Geopolitical Issues on Labor Day 2024." September 2, 2024.
https://www.linkedin.com/pulse/tackling-several-pressing-criminal-justice-issues-labor-maurice-blair-erxuc

Novikov, Illia & Burrows, Emma. "Ukraine's Foreign Minister Kuleba resigns as Russian strikes kill 7 people in Lviv." September 4, 2024. Associated Press.
https://apnews.com/article/ukraine-russia-resign-kuleba-bb5195cc2df40d32bac374ece6dbc0b8

Various news stories from a variety of news outlets corroborated that renowned actor James Earl Jones (1931-2024) died on September 9, 2024.

Orf, Darren. "Earth's Missing 3rd Energy Field Has Appeared in the Arctic Skies." September 9, 2024, 11:35 A.M. U.S. EASTERN DAYLIGHT. *Popular Mechanics*. https://www.popularmechanics.com/science/environment/a62060859/ambipolar-electric-field/

....
....
....
....
....
....
....
....
....
....
....
....

CHAPTER SEVEN 37

In case it proves inconvenient to the reader at any time to pay an online visit the aforementioned article that I posted on September 2, 2024 to LinkedIn yet convenient to visit this chapter of this book, and so as to allow me to augment portions with supplemental comments at several junctures, here is a copy of that article, via portions of screenshots derived from a pdf of it, together with extra, updated commentary presented in red between a few of the original narrative's transitions:

Although likely unknown to the living as of 2 SEP 2024 who the photographer was for that June 15, 1950 photo, by context likely a Blair or a Hoppe.

Tackling Several Pressing Criminal Justice and Geopolitical Issues on Labor Day 2024

Maurice Blair
Multiprofession Worker

38 Simplicity, Intricacy, and Beyond: S.R.P.C., Hypervol. III

September 2, 2024

Although President Bill Clinton became sharply criticized over a quarter of a century ago for the statement, "It depends what your definition of the word 'is' is," and at least one very similarly-worded statement that he made at around the same time, clarification of competing definitions can prove helpful, whether or not you are to any degree whatsoever loyal to the interests of the United States, the American Psychiatric Association, the Democratic Party, the Republican Party, Israel, Iran, Russia, the Ukraine, Citizens Commission on Human Rights, or anyone else.

On Sunday, September 1, 2024, during an interview broadcast by ABC, Senator Lindsey Graham stated, "Hamas could care less about the hostages or the Palestinians..."[1] People could debate and set up a *Family Feud* type of survey in which we ask a random group of people, "On a scale of 1 to 10, how much do you believe that Hamas cares about the people living in Gaza?"

Maybe some already have.

{September 6, 2024 Updated Remark on this: Sometimes I oscillate between a kind of moral agnosticism toward virtually everyone and feeling a sense of direct proof about how we can sometimes know a clear-cut difference between ethical behavior and unethical behavior.}

However, in this case, focus away from that for at least a little while, choosing at least temporarily to let it be that many different people will tend to gravitate toward whatever they believe about this subject; focus instead on your notions of the vast arrays of possible definitions of caring, compassion, attack, defense, ethics, sanity, insanity, and humanity vs. other people's notions of those very same definitions.

A little later, then consider letting whatever your perceptions are about this subject return to you with whichever additional insights arrive.

Whether a given person likes it or not, it makes sense for public figures such as Senator Graham to express their opinions on these matters, and it

CHAPTER SEVEN

makes sense for competing public figures to do so--sometimes cooperating figures, sometimes competing figures such as Representative Alexandria Ocasio-Cortez, Representative Marjorie Taylor Green, Vice President Kamala Harris, Sean Hannity, Al Franken, President Barrack Obama, President George W. Bush, President Donald Trump, HH the 14th Dalai Lama, HH Pope Francis, and Jordan Peterson.

Consider next something adjacent to the cautionary video from Jordan Peterson with the title, "Run Away from DARK TETRAD Types."[2] A ways into the video he focused on how some use a veneer of compassion in order to manipulate others into complicity in conducting vile behavior rooted in selfish pursuits of power, then took this further with his own take on some of the major roots of modern American difficulties.

Relate this again to the idea of competing definitions. Whether a given person thinks of good and evil by framing it in a given way, each and every paradigm of how to define anything and how to model anything or anyone has a huge impact on the beholder's notions.

{Another 06 SEP 2024 Remark adjacent to portions of that article: Neil Young & Crazy Horse's music album *Rust Never Sleeps* (1979) reflects many mysteries of the human condition, by the way. Also, much of the entire *Transformers Franchise* of audiovisual entertainment shares with *Rust Never Sleeps* that recurring emphasis on going beyond the observable, limited appearances to reach toward enhanced awareness of what is or may actually be going on way beyond the surface. That, too, could relate to the excellent 2024 motion picture film *Reagan*.}

We can agree with whichever people we choose to agree with, but to whatever degree we may be turning a blind eye to the reality that other people are truly experiencing, we may be missing not only a boat or a bus, but multiple fleets of many kinds of vehicles.

If you snap reacted to this with something similar to thinking toward me, "Speak for yourself and those who think like you, don't speak of me with being part of your 'we' or 'us'--I am not of like mind with you, I am much better attuned to reality. You and many other people who think like you are clearly of inferior minds and inferior thought patterns. There is no 'we' or 'us' involving you and me. I know much of truth and reality, and you only know much of reality when it hits you hard. I am out of here, and I have no need to know any more of what you are writing with this article. You are beneath contempt, and it shows from what little I already know about you. Get lost! Bye," then, rest assured, be it known that I have already frequently let go of all idea structures in recent years, via zazen and other processes, and I have frequently let select idea structures back at various stages.

Therefore, a main response could be, "If you fix yourself on those notions, then you will largely be swinging wildly with sabre-rattling against empty air until you catch yourself doing that." A brief supplemental case-in-point: I typically write with the American conventions of English spellings, including how "saber-rattling" would be considered standard, yet I intentionally presented it as "sabre-rattling" just now, because the energy of the situation intuited as going better with the British convention than with the American convention on that occasion. (That parallels how in America there are many references to "theater" and rarer references to "theatre.")

This ties in very closely with the idea of getting past ideas.

CHAPTER SEVEN 41

Getting past them, that is, in order to delve further into the core of reality itself, to later emerge more capable of properly coordinating idea structures for the benefit of everyone in the long run.

Some might contend at this stage, "What's the use of bothering to include the phrase 'in the long run,' when, as the late, legendary economist John Maynard Keynes famously pointed out, 'In the long run, we're all dead,' what's the use?"

To those a response could be, "Get past your defensiveness about the idea of the long run; yes, it makes sense to avoid robbing the present in order to support the past and the future, but it can also make sense, at least to some degree on some occasions, to refrain from robbing the past and the future in excessive support of the present."

Another response could be, "Whether you primarily have Jesus Christ, Shakyamuni Buddha, Immanuel Kant, John Maynard Keynes, Arthur C. Clarke, or anyone else involved with your worldview or your multiple worldviews, some level of either your conscious or your subconscious mind has flexibility enough to connect with a sense of at least some amount of long-term cosmic justice being possible. Even if you've castigated as far as you know even a trace of admitting to the possibility of such long-term justice, wait around a while... it will probably come back to you sooner or later as a notion, whether it is by reality hitting you in the face or by some spark of conscience bringing it all back home to your consciousness."

Circling back now to an issue of definitions with how Senator Graham chose to phrase things, notice from the video how he repeatedly used the phrase, "could care less" rather than the alternative "could not care less."

There are many levels to this difference of phraseology, and although some people have tried to define the "could not care less" version as being more correct than the "could care less" version--some television commercial from about the 2009-2013 time period comes to mind--there are clear advantages and disadvantages to both versions.

To state something obvious that the aforementioned TV ad had stated, "could care less" leaves room for the possibility that the amount of caring is greater than some less-caring alternative; therefore, it is not as extreme a statement in some respects.

However, here are three expressions of how "could care less" actually has an advantage over "could not care less" in some applications:

1) In a conversation circa 2010, my late father (Maurice A.T. Blair, who, from my perspective, seems one of the likely candidates for being the correct answer regarding who might have taken the 1950 photograph (of a bear and its surroundings) as appearing near the beginning of this article) received a question from me on this very grammatical issue, and he responded with words to the effect of, "When someone says, 'I could care less,' that could stand for, '*I could care less, but it would take effort for me to care less.* You see, I *could* make the effort to eliminate my caring about it, *but I do not even care enough about the fact that I care so little about it to even bother to take the effort to eliminate that microscopic amount of caring.*"

2) *Ecclesiastes* 7:7-10 (as expressed by the *KJV*) states, "Surely oppression maketh a wise man mad; and a gift destroyeth the heart. Better *is* the end of a thing than the beginning thereof; *and* the patient in spirit *is* better than the proud in spirit. Be not hasty in thy spirit to be angry: for anger resteth in the bosom of fools. Say not thou, What is *the cause* that the former days were better than these? for thou dost not enquire wisely concerning this."

CHAPTER SEVEN   43

Notice that it mentions a gift as in some contexts having a destructive effect. Contrast that with how in a great many contexts this would seem counterintuitive to a great many beholders.

In this case, though, with the phraseology of "could care less" in some cases having a rhetorical advantage over "could not care less," the explanation described in #1 serves as one of the many possible bridges between the scriptural verse and the day-to-day regular world.

Returning to what Lindsey Graham had stated, and coordinating it with the ancient passage referenced, an alternative illustration could be to state, "It would seem to many observers that Hamas' recent actions struck Senator Graham as demonstrating that Hamas cares extremely little about either the vast majority of Israeli Jews or the vast majority of Palestinian Muslims, whereas it cares monomaniacally about its notion of a justified quest for power and influence, and Senator Graham believes Hamas to be

thoroughly excessive in rationalizing to itself that its degree of a quest for power and influence has moral justification. If Hamas did not care at all about hostages and did not care at all about Palestinians, then its actions would go to such an extreme that although it would have brought about righteous indignation from him, it would not have caused him what he called heartbreak--it would not have destroyed much of his heart--the way that it did. This is an example of how a small gift can destroy the heart more than the lack of a gift."

(Conversely, people on different sides of the controversy could make vastly contrasting statements assigning much blame elsewhere, with accusations flying back and forth about who is "monomaniacally pursuing power and influence" and who is "refraining from monomaniacally pursuing power and influence." Rather than step further into directly dealing with that debate, turn attention to other related issues, and, perhaps after this article, return to that debate somewhere beyond this article.)

Another example would be if a hospitality industry professional expects a tip from someone--perhaps at least a 15% tip--and gets stiffed, then it could be less disheartening to that worker than if she/he/it/they were to receive a microscopic tip in the same situation.

Imagine waiting a table for four that runs up a huge tab, and that you perform excellent service without making any mistakes along the way. Imagine after that, that you then get paid in cash with exact change plus, after the exact-change payment in full, the person making the payment on behalf of that party hands over one mere dime to you as tip. Then that person says to you glibly, "Yes, I can spare a dime to tip you," immediately followed by the other three looking at you with contempt and laughing out loud at you to your face.

Although I am not taking sides on the hotel workers strike that is an active situation at the time of this article, I respect that both sides of that controversy are seeking what they believe is proper respect and rightful economic opportunity.[3]

Also, as a practicing Buddhist who at times includes a degree of Esoteric Christianity, Nondenominational Esotericism, and other things with spiritual practices and beliefs, I respect both sides of the conflict between Muslims and Jews, although I believe that outright terrorism can and does often go way too far.

To reiterate a related idea that has been stated many times in recent decades by a large number of speakers and writers, there is also that issue of how different beholders disagree about whom to label a terrorist, whom to label a freedom fighter, whom to label a political extremist, whom to label a narcissist, whom to label a Machiavellian, whom to label a good politician, whom to label a great leader, etc.

3) Another example along similar lines would be if you were starving halfway to death while living as a homeless person, then, seemingly miraculously, you were offered employment that you were told would be legal, ethical, and legitimate, with livable working conditions. At first, you feel great as it includes access to sufficient food and seems a huge improvement.

However, soon you discover that the new employer manipulated the situation, and you start to consider it as barely improving your situation at all.

In such a scenario, you might lament that in the absence of the gift of that new employment you might have found a much better gift of how to improve your life.

CHAPTER SEVEN 45

You could care less about the gift received in that case, yet it makes sense to care about it at least a little, which proves little consolation to you as you try to figure out what to do next. That includes searching for what could possibly provide a more substantial improvement to your life than an unsustainable employment situation.

It can be easy for many people to get fixed notions about using their ideas of good and evil to rage against whichever politicians, nations, ideologies, employees, employers, institutions, or whatever else they believe to be most responsible for the current problems in the world.

However, any cognitive biases that they might bring to the situation could distort their very definitions of each and every component of how they paint to themselves who is good, bad, or whatever else, and to what degree.

As the late business leader Charles T. Munger had expressed in multiple ways and on multiple occasions, distortions in which people tend to excessively favor those whom they favor and excessively disfavor those whom they disfavor are among what people can, with effort, come to recognize, grow out of, and improve themselves by transcending.

One example of a public figure actually expressing such a thing about his own journey of improvement is that in *Dalai Lama Renaissance, Vol. 2: A Revolution of Ideas* (2009), HH the Dalai Lama briefly stated in a group setting to the others present that he sometimes questions his past support for Marxism, wondering if it may have been excessive, wondering to himself if indoctrination he received prior to the time when he fled Chinese communist-controlled territory may have skewed his view on this subject. Also, he expressed a hopefulness that capitalists, socialists, and others can improve their effect on others if they can more completely connect with genuine compassion and genuine wisdom.

Pivot now to how both current main candidates for the U.S. presidency, V.P. Harris and Former (and Possibly Future) President Trump, have shifted their policy stances many times.

{An updated comment: To state something obvious but well worth reflecting upon: The above portion of that Labor Day 2024 article will become dated once the 2024 U.S. Presidential Election happens and the official results become certified. However, there have been many contentious things in recent times, and it might be more prudent to adjust it to stating "if and when" rather than stating "when"—on account of the many tensions both in America and abroad. That being said, I have repeatedly projected to others a genuine belief in portions of the third quarter of 2024 that there would seem probably only about one chance in a million or maybe even less than that of our future somehow lacking any January 2025 United States Presidential Inauguration.}

Such changes by any politician could be generated by genuine improvements in understanding, an intention to accomplish some type of political expediency of garnering more votes, a plot revolving around a concealed agenda, a transparent process of managing good intentions in an earnest attempt at improvement, a mixture of two or more of these, or something else entirely.

This dovetails neatly with returning to part of what Jordan Peterson discussed in the aforementioned analysis video.[2] If we consider anyone who has ever lived and been a real mover and shaker of social institutions, then it can be easy for a given mind to behold such a powerful person as: 1) genuinely benevolent, compassionate, and wise; 2) intending well, yet profoundly misguided; 3) power-hungry, excessively driven by base motives, and presenting a facade of benevolence, compassion, and wisdom; 4) some hybrid of the aforementioned; or 5) something outside the aforementioned.

However, if we let go of all conceptualizations for at least a little while, we might admit to ourselves that something real definitely happened deep within the very being of any given highly influential person who has ever lived, and that something real is definitely happening in this very instant deep within the very being of each and every currently-living highly influential person.

How close or distant a given person during a given interval is with models of evil personalities, how close or distant a given person during a given interval is with models of good personalities, or whatever else: that is something perhaps best to visit and revisit periodically.

To visit and revisit, that is, in part for the purpose of considering whether it could be an improvement to adjust how much favor, disfavor, neutrality, or anything else to bestow upon any of the influential.

Theoretically, some might say that it would be best to round up all of the people who are greedy leaders or at a high risk of ever becoming greedy leaders and throw them all into psychiatric wards, with one form or another of involuntary commitment.[6] Some people use the phrase "involuntary commitment" to mean a formal legal process that involves a given person being found in need of being put away for a minimum of 90 days or another major length of time for being too much of a psychological menace to society; others use the phrase "involuntary commitment" to mean any time that anyone who does not consent to psychiatric treatment becomes forced into it by others, even without any formal legal process, including if the duration of treatment involves only a few days or a week.

This relates to an old adage of unknown origins, though Maurice A.T. Blair was one of those who has said something essentially identical to it out loud before: "If we locked up all the people that the psychiatric industry tells us should be locked up, then we'd have to have half the people put away and the other half serve as guards, then every so often we'd have to have them change out to switch places."[4][5][6]

Whichever amounts of loyalty anyone might feel toward any government, party, organization, movement, or anyone or anything else, opportunities abound for improving one's wisdom, compassion, accuracy, and balance.

Notes:

[1] Cf. https://www.youtube.com/watch?v=JrYwtkGcmOE as accessed on September 2, 2024 (as had also been broadcast by ABC on television on September 1, 2024).

[2] Cf. https://www.youtube.com/watch?v=PY8U7DHW2-Q as accessed on September 1, 2024 and September 2, 2024.

[3] Cf. https://www.cbsnews.com/news/hotel-strike-boston-seattle-hawaii-marriott-hyatt-which-hotels-impacted/ as accessed on September 2, 2024.

[4] Consider that sentiment in comparison and contrast with the song and the music video "People Are Crazy" as performed by Billy Currington. Cf. https://www.youtube.com/watch?v=PKpQRjj_WbU as accessed occasionally over a span of many years, including as accessed on September 2, 2024.

[5] As a very different set of perspectives that could relate to much of this, consider the song "Beware of Darkness" as performed by the late George Harrison. As of Labor Day 2024, at https://www.youtube.com/watch?v=FrsGTltbss4 there appears a manifestation of that.

[6] The motion picture film *Sakharov* (1984) could also serve as a warning that weaves together many of these same themes.

CHAPTER SEVEN

* * * * *

Having completed the presentation of one article, please consider the information in and/or adjacent to the article referenced below, which describes a news story that touches on issues of renewable energy, the environment, economics, and public responsibility.

Campbell, Ben. "For The First Time in 50 Years United States Government Gives Green Light for New Nuclear Reactor." September 5, 2024. Past Chronicle. https://www.pastchronicle.com/for-the-first-time-in-50-years-united-states-government-gives-green-light-for-new-nuclear-reactor/

* * * * *

Another article's reference information is as follows:

McRae, Mike. "We May Already Be Touching The Andromeda Galaxy, Scientist Finds." September 6, 2024. Science Alert.
https://www.sciencealert.com/we-may-already-be-touching-the-andromeda-galaxy-scientists-find

CHAPTER EIGHT: MORE SETS OF PHOTOS & ARTISTIC DESIGNS & NARRATIVES

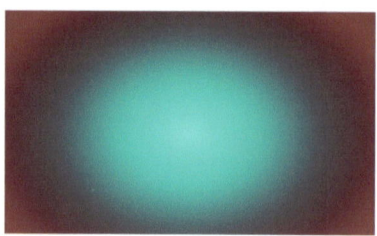

CHAPTER EIGHT

Simplicity, Intricacy, and Beyond: S.R.P.C., Hypervol. III

CHAPTER EIGHT 53

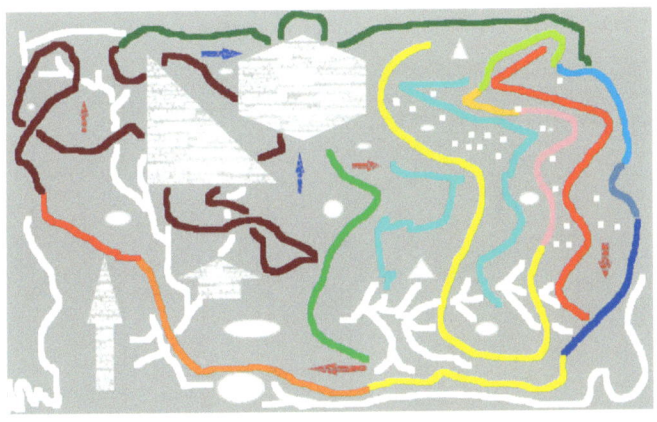

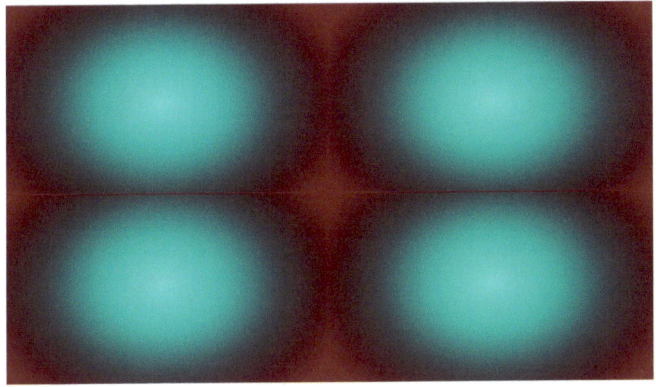

Something that Paramita Bhattacharjee provided to be part of a possible book cover design:

CHAPTER EIGHT

"Maurice James Blair designed this Gateway Pattern in November 2019 and edited it on September 4, 2024"

Chess   Nonchess

Ancient   Modern   Ancient
            Modern

Various   Various

Carlsen

Stockfish   Larsen   Karpov

Beings   Nonbeings

Fischer   AlphaZero
        Kasparov

Reshevsky   Mysteries   Deep
            Blue

Unknowns   Knowns

Capablanca

Ancient   Modern   Ancient
            Modern

Various

Nonchess   Chess

"A Diagram Composed on August 4, 2021, although It Is Unknown If and When An Identical Pattern Might Have Ever Been Arranged Either on Earth or Elsewhere or Both"

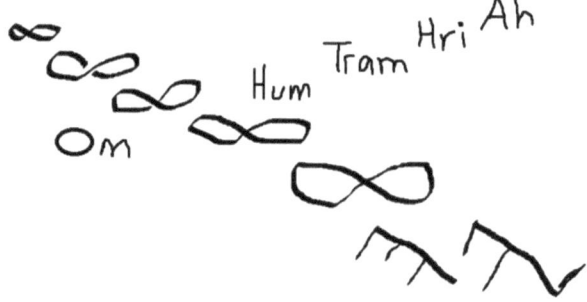

CHAPTER EIGHT

Arriving here is a pattern composed on April 10, 2021:

58 Simplicity, Intricacy, and Beyond: S.R.P.C., Hypervol. III

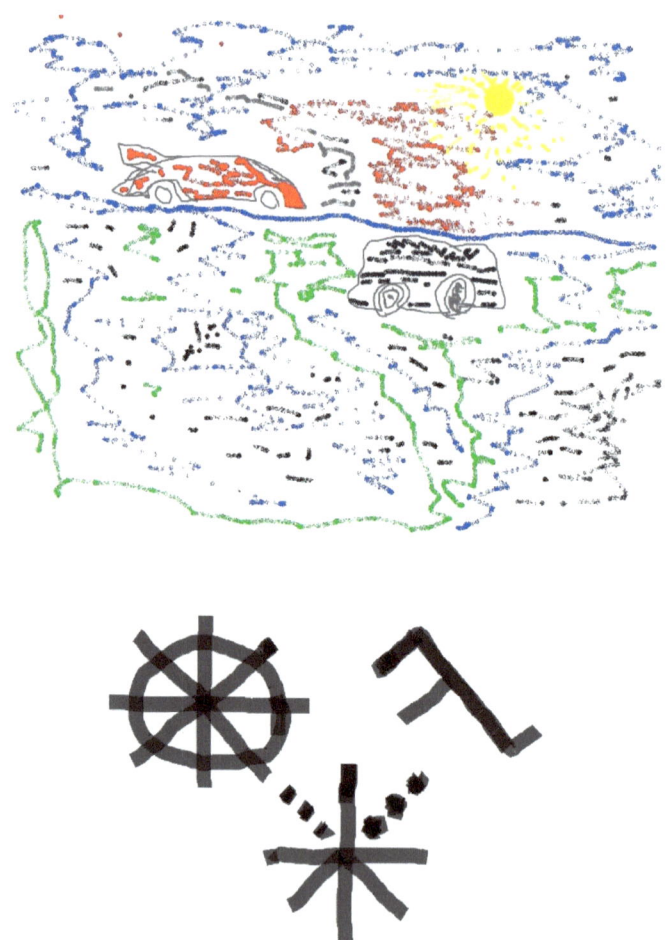

CHAPTER EIGHT

Robin Johnson (of an artistic office in Fleming Island, FL) provided the next design in December 2022:

Paramita Bhattacharjee (of an artistic office in India) provided the following design in March 2024:

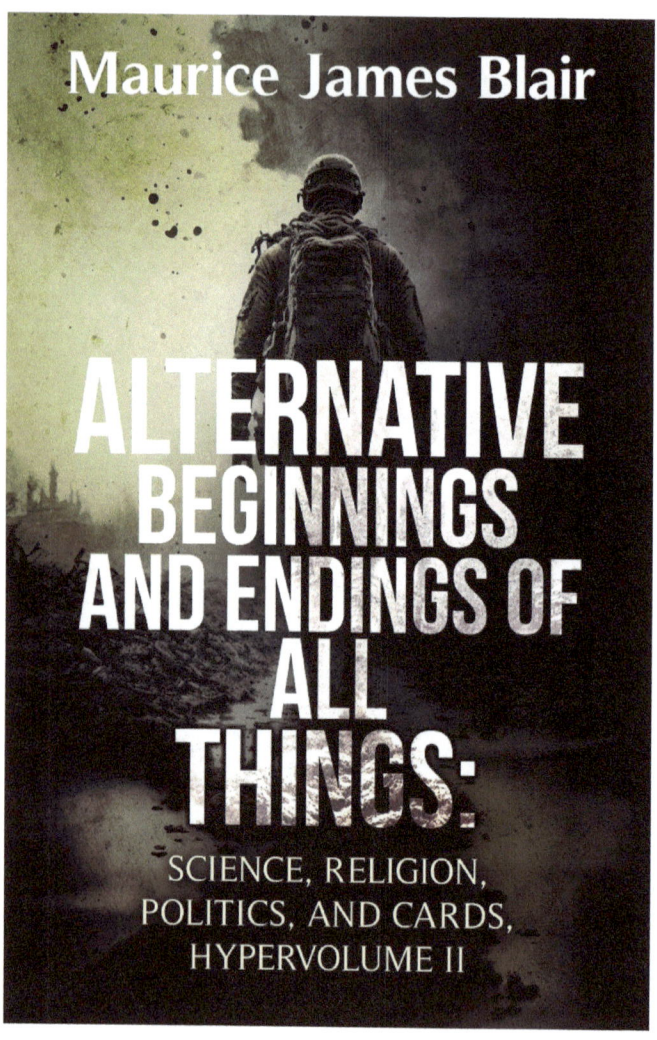

CHAPTER EIGHT

Maurice James Blair, the author of *Simplicity, Intricacy, and Beyond: Science, Religion, Politics, and Cards, Hypervolume III* (2024), created in December 2022 the design seen next:

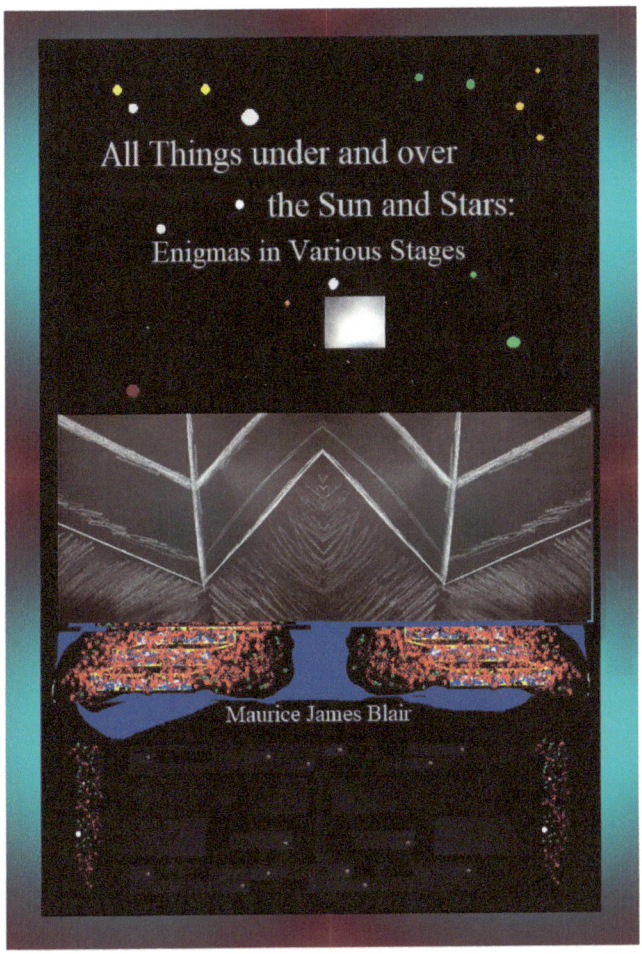

Paramita Bhattacharjee provided this design:

CHAPTER EIGHT   63

A message from M. James Blair, the author of this book, *Simplicity, Intricacy, and Beyond* (2024):

Here is a way in which I organized a multitude of history, philosophy, science, commerce, religion, war, peace, and complexity, into a pattern that I have previously presented to the public elsewhere:

"Civil Uncivil Indigo and More"
(composed on September 7, 2021)

64   Simplicity, Intricacy, and Beyond: S.R.P.C., Hypervol. III

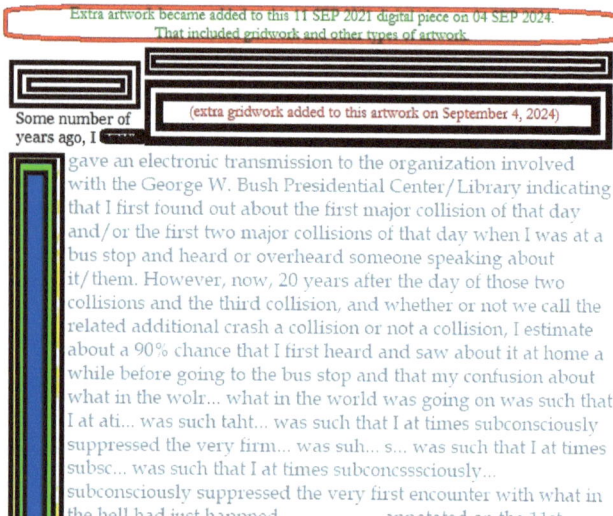

Extra artwork became added to this 11 SEP 2021 digital piece on 04 SEP 2024. That included gridwork and other types of artwork.

Some number of years ago, I ▬▬▬ (extra gridwork added to this artwork on September 4, 2024) gave an electronic transmission to the organization involved with the George W. Bush Presidential Center/Library indicating that I first found out about the first major collision of that day and/or the first two major collisions of that day when I was at a bus stop and heard or overheard someone speaking about it/them. However, now, 20 years after the day of those two collisions and the third collision, and whether or not we call the related additional crash a collision or not a collision, I estimate about a 90% chance that I first heard and saw about it at home a while before going to the bus stop and that my confusion about what in the wolr... what in the world was going on was such that I at ati... was such taht... was such that I at times subconsciously suppressed the very firm... was suh... s... was such that I at times subsc... was such that I at times subconcsssciously... subconsciously suppressed the very first encounter with what in the hell had just happned,... ... ... - annotated on the 11st... annotated on the 11th Day of September of 2021.

CHAPTER EIGHT

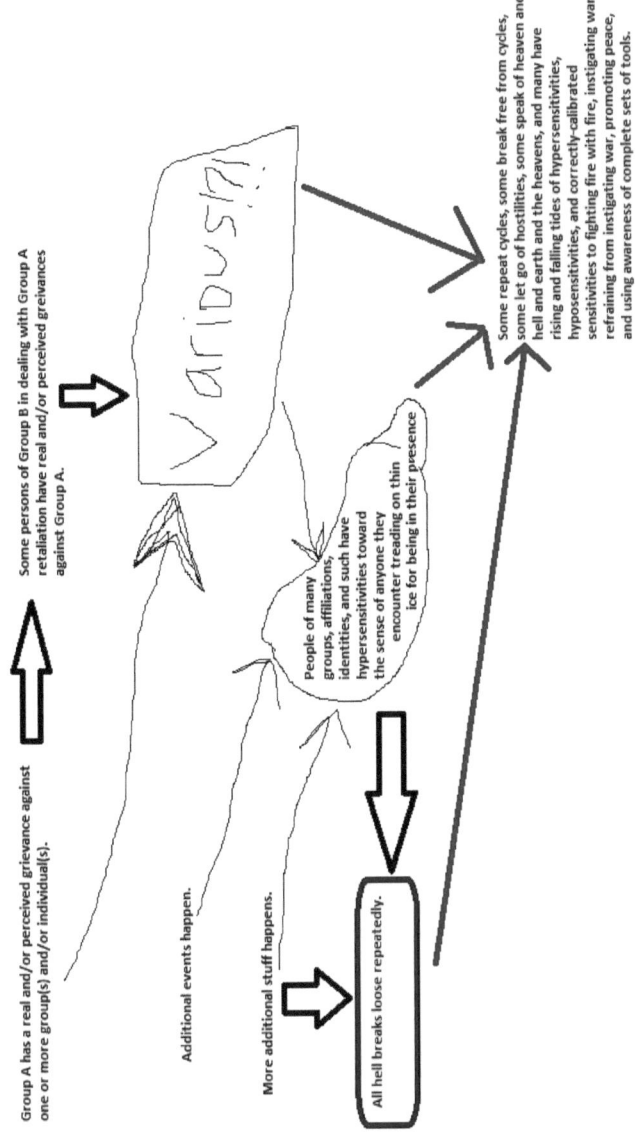

66 Simplicity, Intricacy, and Beyond: S.R.P.C., Hypervol. III

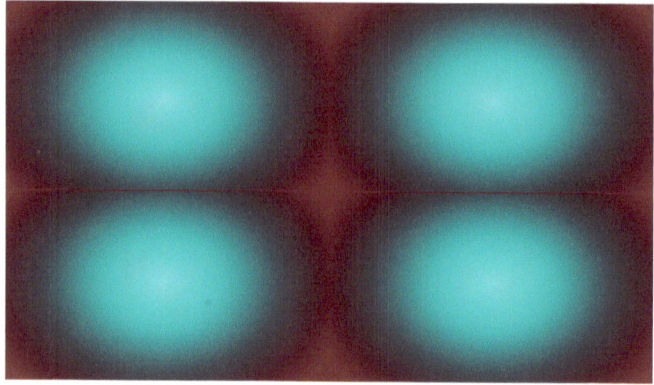

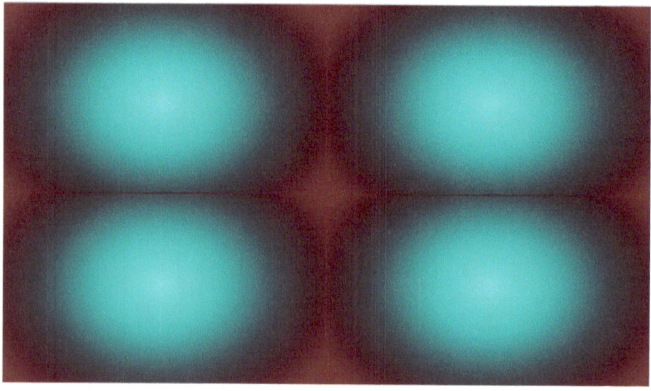

CHAPTER EIGHT

7/26/24, 3:45 PM

People followed by Maurice Blair (@M_James_Blair) / X

Maurice Blair
@M_James_Blair

| Verified Followers | Followers | Following |

Science News ✓
@ScienceNews — (Following)
Covering the latest news in all fields of science. Publisher @society4science. See also @SN_Explores.

Frank McDonald
@FMcDonald_JDS Follows you — (Following)
8th Grade Science Teacher

Wesley Hunt ✓
@WesleyHuntTX — (Following)
Father, Husband, Army Veteran, West Point Graduate, Native Texan. Congressman for TX-38. Follow @RepWPH for Congressional Updates. (American/Apache Pilot)

Elon Musk ✓
@elonmusk — (Following)

Dalai Lama ✓
@DalaiLama — (Following)
Welcome to the official twitter page of the Office of His Holiness the 14th Dalai Lama.

Liza Darnton
@LizaDarnton — (Following)

Simplicity, Intricacy, and Beyond: S.R.P.C., Hypervol. III

7/26/24, 3:34 PM

People following Maurice Blair (@M_James_Blair) / X

Maurice Blair
@M_James_Blair

Verified Followers	Followers	Following

Frank McDonald
@FMcDonald_JDS Follows you
8th Grade Science Teacher
— Following

Bethany Nally
@NallyBetha40138 Follows you
— Follow

Jersey Eitniear
@EitniearJe56354 Follows you
— Follow

Kerrie Conery
@kerr_cone Follows you
✿Kerrie♥22⛳Golf
— Follow

Willow Moor
@MoorWillow49314 Follows you
— Follow

Alicia Hinchey
@hinc_alic Follows you
— Follow

Devora Rambus
@ramb_devor Follows you
🏧21 / My free content 🎤
— Follow

Natividad Fineout
@NatividadF54438 Follows you
— Follow

Pixie Ebe
@pi_ebe Follows you
— Follow

CHAPTER EIGHT 69

Please note that although I feel very good about how I used the Internet to advertise the intention to hire an editor for the development of *All Things under and over the Sun and Stars: Enigmas in Various Stages* (2023) and was able to hire Lee Caleca to fulfil that role, there are several things I wonder about some related things.

First, she and I arranged all of this remotely, and therefore, some might not otherwise know that she and I have only communicated with each other remotely. That is, unless she and I might have ever met without my knowing about her being herself, which seems unlikely given that her profile picture on the freelancing platform and the interactions with her by e-mail all rather clearly point toward her having never met me.

Second, although page 3 of what became the finished product of that work refers to a novel that she wrote many years earlier and which had become published, it seems to be unobtainable for me to read, because 1) repeatedly no copies seem available for purchase or borrowing via any listings on the Internet, 2) Elizabeth Lee Caleca herself told me via email that this has something to do with how she had previously sold rights to it, 3) she is evidently restricted from being able to supply a copy for me to study, and 4) the people with the rights as of late 2022 to early 2023 chose to very much restrict access to it.

Third, although the other work referenced on that work's p. 3, viz. *The Sleeping Giant* (primarily authored by a man named Kam Salami and coauthored by the aforementioned Caleca), is something I have studied small portions of occasionally, as of September 2024 I have only studied a small percentage of it.

Another aspect of that third item is that I have noticed that early in Salami and Caleca's aforementioned 2020 nonfiction book it stepped into an area that a consensus of online authorities as expressed on websites have described as a distortion that is either a conspiracy theory or similar to a conspiracy theory. Namely, that book mentions a controversy involving 432 hertz versus 440 hertz and presents it as closely tied to the legacy of multiple historical atrocities, whereas the article "Debunking social media claims about A=432Hz and A=440Hz musical pitches" (August 2, 2021) by *Reuters Fact Check* presents arguments in favor of exactly what its title indicates it to do. • Cf. https://www.reuters.com/article/fact-check/debunking-social-media-claims-about-a432hz-and-a440hz-musical-pitches-idUSL1N2P915O/

_____

_____

_____

_____

_____

CHAPTER EIGHT

Consider comparing and contrasting a vast array of thoughts, theories, and experiences encompassing the magico-religious realm, the historico-scientific realm, and several combinations and permutations thereof.

_____

_____   _____

_____

For the next two photographs—one of which appears on the next page and another of which appears on the page after that—I am uncertain (as of the time of this book's first going to print) exactly who had taken those photos.

The image on the next page states itself to be from the United States Army, yet it does not specify what person (or persons) served as the photographer(s). The scanning device added a wavy, ghastly effect previously absent from the source copy.

CHAPTER EIGHT

Next, here is a copy of what is almost definitely a 1952 photograph of Howard Bradley (1918-2014) and his significant other Julia (1926-2020). Julia Blair's parents were my paternal grandparents. Her name changed to Julia Bradley upon her marriage to Howard Bradley.

Uncle Howard worked federally at a high level of GS. Aunt Julia worked in banking. They raised a family in California in the 20th century.

74   Simplicity, Intricacy, and Beyond: S.R.P.C., Hypervol. III

Here is a scan of the back side of the photo shown on the previous page:

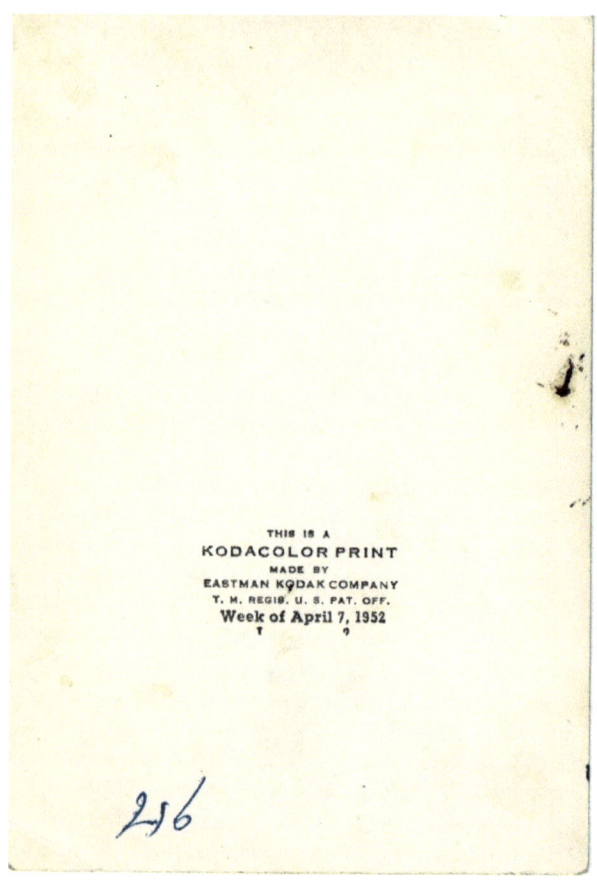

CHAPTER EIGHT

An April 26, 2021 View of Houston, Texas

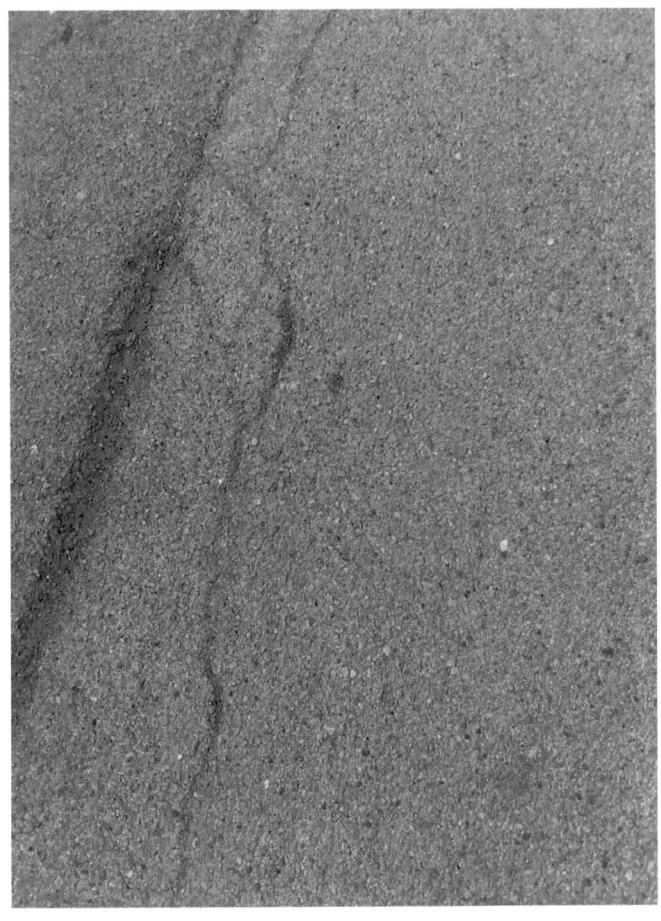

An April 26, 2021 View of Houston, Texas and Some of the Skies Above

Although this work does not include much of the content of the seven attachments to the forwarded e-mail message of the next few pages, a deep awareness of portions of their content and much of their essence is obtainable via a study of a combination of the two previous works in *The Science, Religion, Politics, and Cards Trilogy.*

CHAPTER EIGHT

(An e-mail to: Dr. Ann Blair; cc: Liza Darnton {who served at Penguin years earlier} and Jim Blair {the Maurice James Blair whom Liza met in Durham in 1995; including an alternative e-mail address of the sender w/ the cc.}

Select Information For The Record

Maurice Blair ... Fri, Oct 28, 2022, 4:03 PM
to Ann, Liza, Jim

Dr. Blair,

Although I previously thought that I would never have a reason to contact you, that changed within a span of a few seconds or a few minutes yesterday late afternoon or early evening. I had presumed from records that the communication that I sent to ten recipients, of which Liza Darnton was one, had occurred smoothly enough that I would probably never again contact Liza directly unless she would initiate new direct contact with me. Additionally, I had presumed that the weight of factors on the side of ever initiating first contact with you vs. factors on the side of never initiating first contact with you would probably remain on the side of never contacting you during the remainder of my life.

However, it turned out that Liza's recent former employer, after receiving the letter set on October 3rd and receiving the book on October 17th, decided on October 24th to return to sender the letter set, marking over with labels including "Addressee Unknown," "ATTEMPTED - NOT KNOWN," and "UNABLE TO FORWARD." It appears that they did not open the package or meddle with its contents.

Of all the choices I could make about what to do with that package (returned yesterday), I have decided to do a combination of a) sending you this email and placing both Liza and myself on the cc line and b) sending a package via USPS priority mail with two copies of the first run printing of a hardcover book, two copies of the second run printing of a hardcover book, and four copies of the first run printing of a paperback book. One copy of

(a copy of that October 28, 2022 e-mail message—
"Select Information For The Record"—cont'd)

the second printing of *The Dimetrodons, the Dorians, and the Modern World* is intended for you to eventually give to Liza, to replace the copy that her former employer received on October 17th (signed for by "D.GEER" / 3:43 PM) and which she almost definitely has not and will not ever receive from that organization. The other seven are intended for you to choose where and/or to whom they should go. (That could be almost anywhere, even twenty-five feet underground without a marker.) Of course, with your being on leave and with all other factors, for all I know, you or Harvard just might wind up sending the entire package back to me, kind of like how Amazon.com sent the much smaller package contained within it back to me. I believe that course of action probably would not be anywhere near optimal, yet with the way that many things have gone with some individuals and organizations in recent years, I would not be surprised if that turns out to be what happens.

As a side note, I shall briefly mention that during my junior year of high school (1992-1993) I was accepted by both the Harvard summer session 1993 program and a Baylor summer session 1993 program, and I chose to take two classes with the Baylor program, turning down Harvard; it was probably for the best, because my interpersonal skills at the time were somewhat passable for Baylor University and were probably nowhere near passable for Harvard University. Of course, there could still be some folks here and there who would at times allege that my recent and current interpersonal interactions do not fully qualify me to be a human being, yet I know that some major percentage of people (who either know or know of me) believe that my recent and current interpersonal interactions do fully qualify me to be a human being.

As another aside, addressing an obvious question, to the best of my knowledge, if you and I share any portions of ancestry, it would probably be many generations back.

CHAPTER EIGHT

(a copy of that October 28, 2022 e-mail message—
"Select Information For The Record"—cont'd)

You might wonder at this stage why the message and the sending of the books. The attachments to this email help with clarifying major portions of those whys, and here is a brief supplemental explanation of portions of why:

1) After my health had a major catastrophe in 1996, I often mainly aimed to get by with life rather than aiming for anything lofty, yet additional challenges happened, sometimes leading to reinstigating lofty aims. At this time, I am neither primarily aimed at the lofty level nor the getting-by level; rather, my life's recently generally with an aim to get the ultimate levels of reality to work well from the most all-encompassing perspectives.

2) I felt fine about letting go of things like being very vocal or putting together large amounts of written communication in many portions of mid-2008 to August 4th, 2019, yet people who repeatedly chose a degree of picking a fight with me in the November 21st, 2018 to July 2019 period without yet crossing redlines started to cross those redlines on August 5th, 2019 in their interactions with me. I had already premeditated around 6 AM Central on December 15th, 2018 that if they would ever cross some of those redlines, then I would get to the brink of going thermonuclear on them. On August 5th, 2019 I gave what I considered sufficient warning to them that they were within a few feet or a few millimeters of my unleashing war on them, yet they proceeded as of around 5 PM August 6th, 2019 to crossing the final redline to where I declared war on them. Not war of physically-fully-manifested nukes but of interpersonal, interorganizational, and interfaith nukes.

(OCT 2022 "Select Information For The Record"—cont'd)

3) The countless hours of conversations that I had with Joel Edward Goza from about December 2004 to mid-2005 in some ways presaged the later 2018-2021 conflicts with varieties of people of various races, religions, and other demographics, and, as you might see if you look at the nonprofit/for-educational-purposes for-book-printing Word file "Of Dorians R H W D R I & Beyond 2022 03 07.docx" (which I give you and others with access to it permission to copy and print on the condition of refraining from altering it in any way), I included that Joel on the cc line of a couple of messages in which I argued ferociously with James Liptrap in latter portions of August 2021. Since the time of composing that March 7th, 2022 book, I have moved somewhat more toward the center politically (though in many respects still very much on the conservative side), yet it captures for eternity vantages on much of what led up to that date and portions of what was of that date in history. Sometimes I felt that it would be best to do a second edition of that book, to reflect moving to a degree toward the center, yet I later changed my mind and decided that creating a new fiction book with many of the same themes and elements would be even better.

4) The most pointed conversation between Joel Goza and myself while we were both employees of KPMG, a conversation that happened either at the Flying Saucer restaurant in downtown Houston or a similar place, approximately February or March 2005, was one in which he argued that on the basis of some Gospel teachings along the lines of "Render unto Caesar that which is Caesar's, render unto God that which is God's" (for example, Cf *Matthew* 22:21), he believed that The Founders of The United States of America were illegitimate in their choice to conduct The Revolutionary War, and I argued back that (with or without taking those Gospel teachings into account) I believed that The Founders of The United States of America were legitimate in their choice to conduct The Revolutionary War.

5) Regarding the characterization I presented to Liza in one of the pdfs, I subsequently changed my mind to a tentative plan that if and when I put together a full-length autobiographical manuscript, then and there I may first pursue the normal large-scale approach of contacting literary agents and such. If that fails to gain traction, then I will consider alternate options for bringing publication to fruition, including both for-profit approaches and not-for-profit approaches.

CHAPTER EIGHT

(OCT 2022 "Select Information For The Record"—cont'd)

As a footnote, something which I declined to include as a pdf was correspondence in which I incorrectly referred to receiving 21st-Century e-mail communications from Dorsey Armstrong in 2009 and 2019, then separately corrected for Kathleen Larkin Spires and Dorsey Armstrong that the years were 2010 and 2019. I had left it to Liza to eventually likely find out via reading page 90 of the complimentary book I sent her via Lulu Publishing; whereas I refrained from sending a complimentary copy of that book to either Larkin or Dorsey.

Now, from where I stand, there is possibly a major likelihood that Liza might not ever obtain that book, and, therefore, whether or not this turns out to be the last direct communication she receives from me, I believe it best to give her the likely correcting of her awareness of that detail, in case any butterfly/ripple/domino effects emanating from that might work better for her well-being (and perhaps also for the well-being of all other sentient beings) in the long run.

Although I refrained from including with this e-mail message the five attachments to the August 4th, 2022 autobiographical e-mail message, there are excerpts from the first three in portions of the aforementioned hardcover book, and, theoretically,it might be possible for either Liza or me to someday forward that message to you.

> I am not seeking any direct response from either you or Liza in sending this to you and cc'ing her; neither do I expect it likely to receive such a response. That being said, I hope that neither you nor Liza decide to go on a path of attacking me in response to my acts of sending this message and the related shipment, though I am willing to accept that risk as part of what I believe to be my duty to reality.
>
> Regards,
>
> M.J. Blair
>
> **7 Attachments**

Comments on that October 28, 2022 e-mail message:
- As mentioned on p. 73 of *Science, Religion, Politics, and Cards*, I actually sent a December 2009 e-mail message to Dr. Armstrong, yet in that message I expressed a little bit of doubt about whether my memory was correct about her having been the instructor from years earlier whom I thought her to be. In March 2010 I sent an email to her that reflected that certainty had returned to my memory that she was indeed the instructor who over a decade and a half earlier had been in grad school and teaching a class of undergrads who had included me.
- In Q3 of 2024 up to the time of finalizing the text of this work for first printing, I have usually been leaning against creating any new manuscripts to send to literary agents, believing that something about my place in reality might be a solid and immovable obstacle against being marketable enough as a writer for it to make sense for any literary agent to wish to have me as a client. You might wonder why I bother to continue with creating a modest amount of literature, rather than walking away from it yet. Of the many reasons, one of them is to tie up loose ends that could otherwise be problematic for the future of what information is readily available to some range of sentient beings. Another is that I perceive it to be a very realistic possibility that someday living,

biological entity human beings may become extinct while intelligent, living, biological entities who might be extraterrestrial, interdimensional, a mixture of the two, etc. might benefit from having these as an additional record of what in the universe/multiverse had been going on with those weird beings the humans. Yet another still is that I feel much more interested in how my investment of time, money, and effort into the creation of literature might help with the future for after I die than I do with if a similar amount of time, money, and effort went into building some grand burial mausoleum on some plot somewhere. Much of this stuff could provide extra clues and insights into what in the world went on with a bunch of people and places and whoever and whatever else. Of course, I recognize that some detractors may easily jump to some conclusion of accusing the entire process as an act of vanity and/or narcissism and a waste of time for everyone and everything. However, to closely parallel Liz Phair (in "Divorce Song"), I'll let you know that I do not consider you, no matter who you might be, to be a waste of time and space to the human race, even if you have already been rightfully convicted of a heinous crime and are in your last minutes before execution.

Imagine that scenario, if you will. If that's the case, then I believe that you can still help the future, even if the best way is for you to face the electric chair, guillotine, scaffold and rope, lethal injection, firing squad, or whatever else in a way that you can somehow—right there near the end—change the future trajectory of your effect on everyone else to become more into the direction of being for the good, the great, the better, the greater, or maybe even the very best.

This discussion has suddenly reminded me of that excellent movie *The Green Mile* (1999).

Another thought occurred to me at about 6:40 A.M. Houston, TX time on Tuesday, September 10, 2024. However, I shall decline to mention here in this book exactly what type of inspiration for transformation and teamwork it involves. Suffice it to say, if you someday wind up with a need to know that idea pattern, then maybe someday you will find it, whether from a chain reaction emanating from me, a chain reaction emanating from some public figure from long ago, or from another source, etc.

CHAPTER EIGHT

Part of What Became Visible on X in the First Half of August 2024, with Sidebar Options Rearranged to Show Three of Them Near the Top of the Display:
(reformatting of portions of image & adding of title: September 4, 2024)

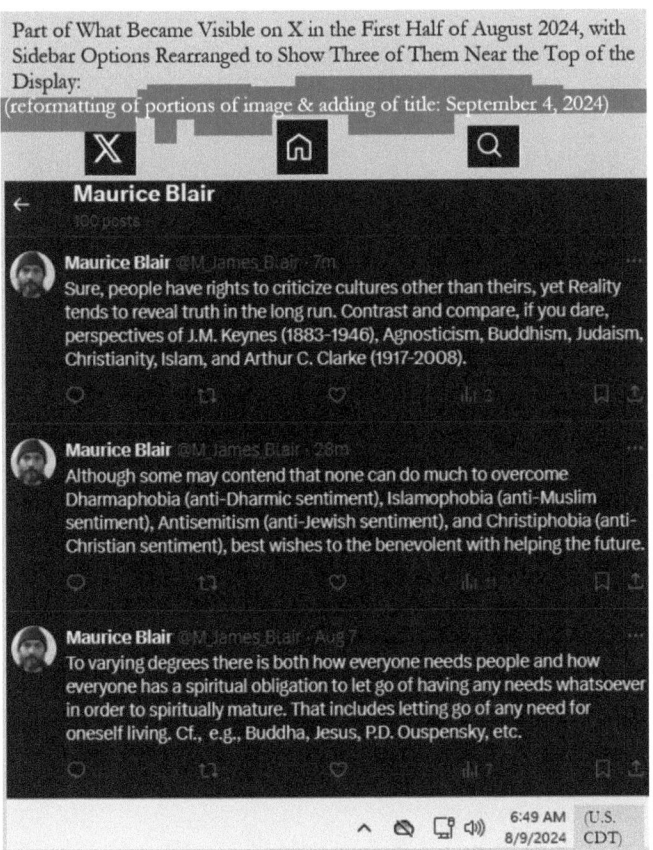

On May 15, 2024, I took the photograph presented here. More information regarding it is included in *Alternative Beginnings and Endings of All Things* (2024).

CHAPTER EIGHT

According to platform records, IFLScience posted to Facebook on August 31, 2024 a digital image that led to an online discussion between Jeff Hancock and others (after he reposted it). A rearranged copy (with proportions of text adjusted for legibility) is here:

I responded to Jeff Hancock's act of reposting of it by referring to consider when "Reality flexes" such as to blur boundaries between science, religion, and science fiction.

Jeff then indicated he lacked experiential evidence of "reality flexing." As reflected by the partial screenshots copied to the next couple of pages, I then answered with references to experiences, TV, and changing thoughts.

88   Simplicity, Intricacy, and Beyond: S.R.P.C., Hypervol. III

Part of a screen from about 4:55 PM U.S. CDT on 01 SEP 2024:

Maurice James Blair
Jeff Hancock Great, but I have on many occasions experienced waking life become indistinguishable from as if I were from within being a fictional character in some of the science fiction scenarios in which it does such flexes. This could relate to how the July 27, 1989 Clarke introduction to the 1990 adjusted version of CHILDHOOD'S END (1953) includes a statement that although he believed the vast majority of claims to paranormal events are bunk, "it can't *all* be nonsense." (The italicized "all" in the referenced text was adjusted into "*all*" here.) In many of his later decades he leaned heavily toward an almost uniform skepticism, yet he did occasionally express at least a little openness toward some extremely profound possibilities happening in real-life. Blowing off all of it by saying that any experiences of major reality flexes have to be from people experiencing mental illness also does not explain it away for people--whether having ever been officially deemed insane by any medical professionals or not--who wind up directly experiencing such things. People who have never experienced such things might best be extremely skeptical until if and when they directly experience such things. Some people are confident that we all get to experience such things after we die, other people are not quite so sure. However, I have experienced some of them in this life. Eventually, I chose to occasionally mention some of these in writing, including in a few portions of some books I wrote or cowrote. Also, there was a TV show from the late 20th century called BEYOND BELIEF: FACT OR FICTION (consider visiting https://www.imdb.com/title/tt0138956/... for reference) that played up this issue in an entertaining format. Back when I watched that show ahead of having had such experiences, I often thought along the lines of, "Are any of the purportedly factual stories out of the mixture presented actually factual or are all of them simply made up by people?" Later, I came to recognize, "Yep, since I've experienced some of those kinds of things directly, yes, it seems overwhelmingly probable (to me, at least) that at least some small sliver of people historically have also experienced Reality flex in such ways on at least a few occasions. It does not guarantee that any more than a small sliver of claims to the paranormal are real, but it does give me confidence that at least some very small percentage, maybe less than one percent, or maybe some different percentage, of the most extraordinary claims from human history are based on actual, factual, extraordinary events.

IMDB.COM
Beyond Belief: Fact or Fiction (TV Series 1997–2024)
7.9 | Mystery, Thriller, Fantasy

3m   Like   Reply   Remove Preview

Regarding that set of perspectives, I clarified some aspects a few days later.

CHAPTER EIGHT

entertaining format. Back when I watched that show ahead of having had such experiences, I often thought along the lines of, "Are any of the purportedly factual stories out of the mixture presented actually factual or are all of them simply made up by people?" Later, I came to recognize, "Yep, since I've experienced some of those kinds of things directly, yes, it seems overwhelmingly probable (to me, at least) that at least some small sliver of people historically have also experienced Reality flex in such ways on at least a few occasions. It does not guarantee that any more than a small sliver of claims to the paranormal are real, but it does give me confidence that at least some very small percentage, maybe less than one percent, or maybe some different percentage, of the most extraordinary claims from human history are based on actual, factual, extraordinary events.

IMDB.COM

Beyond Belief: Fact or Fiction (TV Series 1997–2024) ⭐ 7.9 ...

3d   Like   Reply   Remove Preview

 Maurice James Blair
Clarification upon memories of old episodes of that improving: The "all" I referred to was not of "fact ones" that might be "explainable by remote coincidence together with normal science," but "fact ones" that "seemed to defy normal science."

1m   Like   Reply

4:14 PM
9/5/2024

CHAPTER EIGHT

91

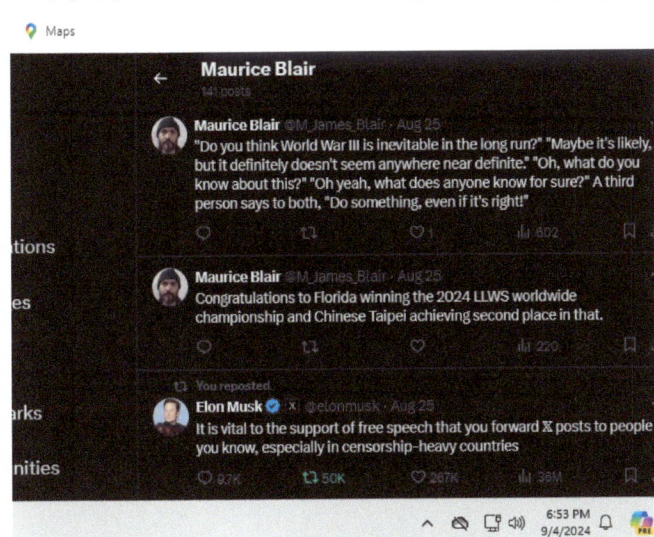

A transcription with font adjustments for effect, forwarding several August 25, 2024 platform X statements:

• Elon Musk: It is vital to the support of free speech that you forward X posts to people you know, especially in censorship-heavy countries.

• Maurice Blair: Congratulations to Florida winning the 2024 LLWS worldwide championship and Chinese Taipei achieving second place in that.

• Maurice Blair: "Do you think World War III is inevitable in the long run?" "Maybe it's likely, but it definitely doesn't seem anywhere near definite." "Oh, what do you know about this?" "Oh yeah, what does anyone know for sure?" A third person says to them, "Do something, even if it's right!"

Here is the beginning of how J.H. had several things inaccurate while attacking me by Facebook Messanger on September 8, 2024, and how I answered him. - M.J.B.

Justin Haynes
Active 24m ago

1:59 PM

You're an idiot. Why give everything away to rich bitch asshole who doesn't even care if you're alive or dead. 🖕

People are literally living in poverty and you want to make a rich bitch asshole richer.

You literally watch me drown in poverty and don't even give a fuck, yet some rich bitch who isn't even your friend is your beneficiary?

Leave your shit to charities that help people not make a rich bitch richer.

I don't want to be your beneficiary or your fucking money 💰 I'm just saying it grates my soul.

Play you're my friend and you just literally just watched me drown and wash out and and get evicted but then you turn around and some fuck stranger comes along and you fucking help them but not your own friend. Kind of hurts my feelings.

Anyways, I've always come through and helped you whenever I could even though I didn't have much and you've never really returned the favor so I think this friendship needs to fucking end

11:00 PM
9/8/2024

CHAPTER EIGHT

> From a September 8-9, 2024 debate between Justin Haynes and me (Maurice J. Blair). Screenshot 2, which includes an early part of the initial Maurice James Blair response (my initial response) to the attack that Justin had presented. screenshot 2 within this chronicle of that debate

5:27 PM

Justin, I've helped you several times, and I worked hard toward helping you when you had the recent problem when you were forced out by your father, yet a combination of my mother Ming and concern for a water leak in the kitchen plus the coincidence of the repairman's schedule and the timing of your problem became too much of a roadblock in my estimation that day, then Erica ended up helping you that time, as I heard. Then eventually, you had trouble with her again, and your father at least partway reconciled with you and helped you, and you moved back in with him. Whatever your current situation, consider choosing wisely if you can. Back on that day when I

11:03 PM 9/8/2024

ended up not going over to help you get your stuff out of your father's house, one of the things that weighed on me also was that there was both an indication (from either you or ▮▮▮ or both) that there was a restraining order for you to not go near that house at that time and an indication (from you) that you were going to that house and that there was not really any restraining order. On top of the other problems, that contradiction gave me some pause. Also, I tried to get ▮▮▮▮▮▮▮▮▮▮▮▮▮▮▮ to go over there to help you get your stuff from your father's house that day, and I tried getting Crystal Brown (a.k.a. the person with the Facebook ID of Radically Transformed, who is generally willing to consider helping people as part of her belief in Christianity, and who was one of my former employment supervisors from when she and I were both working for Goodwill Houston) to help you out, and neither of them were able to help you that day according to what they told me over the phone during that window of time that you were frantically searching

Screenshot 3 of a presentation of a September 8-9, 2024 debate; here I redacted an abbreviated real identifier and a real name identifier for a mutual friend of Justin's and mine: the E92P-alias man (as labeled by SRPC (2023)).

for help. Yes, my mother's forcefulness of trying very hard to dissuade me from going over and getting into the middle of whatever difficulty was going on between you and your father was a large part of my decision, but no, it was not her decision in the end for me to stay home and wait for the repairman; I weighed all factors and attempted to make the best decision I could in the situation, and it was to avoid going over to that house. Shifting now to another subject: No, I am not leaving all my stuff to Liza, although you misinterpreted that from something or another or someone or another some combination of things and/or beings. And, btw, when I have taken you to meals and covered the cost that was even with knowing ahead of time that upon it almost definitely coming up in conversation with my mother later I would be honest if asked and that it would almost definitely lead to her complaining repeatedly, excessively, and forcefully about why I didn't make some major attempt to have you pay for your own meal each time, despite the wealth disparity. OK, so you stated, "Anyways, I've always come through and helped you whenever I could even though I didn't have much and you've never really returned the favor so I think this friendship need to fucking end." WTF???!!!!! When you snap into something like that from out of the blue, after I've generally been quite reasonable and often have helped some here and there, that exemplifies the kind of thing that Reese told me about around four months ago (approximately May 2024) that you have a serious issue of how you easily wind up having your memories of past traumas lead you to excessively teeing off on people you are currently dealing with once you associate something that happens between them and you with something else from before that happened between someone else and you. If you want to unfriend me, go for it, make my day; I already made it clear to anyone who would listen carefully about it that at a core level I feel fine about human extinction at any instant, and I've felt that quite often since around January 5, 2023; the end of any given friendship is not way too much to handle. You think I think excessively

CHAPTER EIGHT 97

highly of Liza, do you? I'll let you know several developments, around early October 2022 I sent an email to a Harvard professor who had replaced her uncle as a high level history professor there and included her on the cc line, and I communicated a huge amount of the truth of things critical toward both major political parties and invited them to consider carefully. Part of that included a complete electronic copy of the main original file used for the first printing of the nonprofit, nonfiction booklet *Of Dorians, Romans, Hebrews, Whigs, Democrats, Republicans, Indians, and Beyond* (2022). To reiterate, I invited them to consider carefully. Consider carefully, that is, because (as would have been abundantly clear to them from reading between the lines) I had turned the corner: Although there was a period from a few months from mid-2022 to early fall that year when I had a hypersensitivity about Liza such that a direct attack from her would have likely extremely hurtful and troubling to me (and, thankfully, she chose not to directly attack me in any way during that time), by the time I sent that e-mail message to History Professor Ann M. Blair of Harvad and to Liza

> Darnton (whose Uncle Robert had retired such as to replaced by that Dr. Ann Blair), I felt ready that if either that Dr. Blair or that Highly Accomplished Book Editor Darnton were to have sent a hostile e-mail message to me {in a similar vein to what William Crockett Walker (a.k.a. Bill Walker) had done multiple times, to what *Michael Berry Show* assistant Emily Bull had done once, and to what you have done with your recent message to me (to which this is a response)}, then I would have in righteous indignation teed off onto whichever of them would have done so (or both if they would have both dared to do so). However, even with how both of them could have easily found some rationale for attacking me in response to providing them such a large amount of historical perspective about what had transpired leading up to then, including anything they might have otherwise found disagreeable, they chose to remain silent, and I respected that as within the range of very reasonable responses. However, I also believe that your attack on me in this case could be for the best, because, as misguided as it is, it did a combination allowing you to vent some

Screenshot 7 of a debate in which I, Maurice J. Blair, answered a written, verbal attack from Justin Haynes; initial attack was on 8 SEP 2024, initial responses 8-9 SEP 2024.

Note: the Emily hostile message (from April 2023) and the Justin hostile messages (from September 2024) had been after the referenced informative M.J.B. October 28, 2022 message.

CHAPTER EIGHT 99

(another part of how I responded to a September 8, 2024 written attack from a friend on Facebook Messanger) (Note: E92P's real name again redacted.)

of what you honestly thought and felt within your impressions of the situation, and it afforded me an opportunity to give you this response. Also, I rather suspect that you have not yet bothered to find out much, if anything, about and read the article at https://www.linkedin.com/pulse/tackling-several-pressing-criminal-justice-issues-labor-maurice-blair-erxuc (which is something in which I publicly presented a mixture of sharp criticism and opportunities for praise and growth toward all or nearly all beings--past, present, future, and/or beyond). I do not know how much distortion that the aforementioned ▆▆▆▆ may have presented you recently, and I do not know how much accuracy that ▆▆▆▆ may have recently presented to you, but if you will bother to read that article, genuinely study it, and consider other stuff adjacent to it, then you will possibly recognize that I criticized all or nearly all people who have ever lived, no matter what party affiliations if any and whichever socioeconomic conditions they have ever had, and, yes, I also opened the gateways into praise and possible improvement being available to anyone or anything deserving any amount of praise via how there are many escape clauses and springboards within the

(redacting to limit dissemination of E92P's identity)

> structure of that article. My mother often speaks in ways of blasting you and ▮▮▮▮▮▮▮▮▮▮▮▮▮, even though I often feel a moderate favorability toward both you and him in a variety of ways and generally consider both him and you to be among my friends. She also often harshly criticizes me for paying attention sometimes to both you and him, sometimes helping both him and you out, and related stuff. She often tells me that she believes me to do way too much for you and for him. I argue back strongly in most cases regarding this. On another note, before your email message I had tentatively thought about including you as being in the list of people I would suggest to my estate planning attorney as a person who my next of kin might consider hiring after I am dead to serve as a co-executor of my will (the first official version of which will probably become finalized and signed later this month), if you happen to be alive and available at the time and turn out to be able to reach a negotiated agreement with my next of kin for how much to pay you per hour. Although there is a remote chance that I might still consider you for that, your message seems to make it

CHAPTER EIGHT

(the next part of my initial response on September 8, 2024 to Justin's verbal attack by Facebook Messenger from earlier that day - Maurice James Blair, Houston, TX)

clear that you feel that you don't want anything to do with getting help from me in general in the present and the future, unless you change your mind at some stage to feel more favorable toward me again. Fine, you seek to get nothing when you are otherwise on track to possibly get something, and you can easily be adjusted into being on a path toward getting nothing. Yes, I may consider some very remote possibility of bringing that idea back, but before your tirade in that recent Facebook Messenger direct message to me, I had several times in the past week felt certain that I would soon get around to sending an email to that attorney with an idea from me that you should be in that list. Now I am almost certain that whichever way communications with you proceed from here, your chances of that will be either absolute zero or only a little greater than absolute zero. On another note, I spoke briefly with Ustinya about some of your difficulties about a year ago, hoping that this might lead to some improvement for your life, and she had suggested that you could go and visit her then at the Houston mission at which she was then working, and even if you would not be able to pay anything more than five dollars for a small booklet or whatever, that you would then at least be able to benefit from visiting, considering other perspectives, and such. I also told you

(as with some previous references in this set, a variation of E92P's real name has been redacted from this screenshot)

about that back then, and you expressed some mixture of mild interest and much hesitancy. Also, although she is involved with Scientology, several people, including both the aformentioned ▇▇ and myself, have suggested other religous groups that you might benefit from at least lightly checking out... or, if you have already previously checked them out, then lightly checking out anew. Your post from somethink like an-hour-and-a-half-or-two ago or thereabouts on Facebook--a post in which you wonder about your family members often turning you away from fulfilling your requests for their help while they are very open to helping select strangers--seems to reflect the old general rule and adage idea, "Familiarity breeds contempt." Some of them have grown used to thinking with a mixture of thoughts and feelings toward you and of having many interactions with you, and they have settled in on feeling a high degree of contempt for you. Now, with your recent message, you seem to be doing the same thing toward me that you were complaining about some of your close family members doing to you, except that I am not actually seeking any specific help from you; rather, as with almost anyone I set out to interact with, I am seeking for the collaboration to be for the benefit of all sentient beings, in terms of enhancing gateways to spiritual enlightenment, conscience, improvement,

(a continuation of a copy of a Maurice Blair response to a Justin Haynes, involving a September 8, 2024 debate via Facebook Messenger)

etc. However, I am in a state of such peace and grace and resilience that your lashing out at me is something that I can respond to calmly, as I am now. You, like almost everyone who is reasonably alive and reasonably capable, may have great opportunity to eventually turn things around and get better. Sometimes you may need help from people, and some may let you down many times. There are times you might need to find something that makes a huge difference by helping yourself, too, of course; and, there is hope that some people will help you sometimes in the future when you need it. Perhaps you should revisit both the Nine Inch Nails version of "Hurt" and the Johnny Cash version of "Hurt" and think somewhat more about several things involving whichever people you have ever let down, whichever people have ever thought that you let them down although you currently think that they were off base for thinking that you had let them down, whichever people you think have let you down yet which if you could step outside of whatever you might be currently believing about the interactions, then you might find to be people you would come to realize did not actually let you down--or who might have let you down to a lesser degree than you previously were of the impression they had been--(consider that it might be the case, if you will), and which people have actually, very clearly and very definitely let you down in a very big way. Also, you could recognize that interpreting some of these things may depend on interpretations and be involved with many gray areas of how to best think of them. On another note, somewhere beyond issues of whether people believe in any given religion, any combination of religions, or in no religion, here is a reminder that long ago in at least one interview, Johnny Cash said of himself and of June Carter Cash in comarison and contrast with anyone who might listen about it, something that was either word-for-word or nearly word-for-word amounting to the statement, "You have a choice in life to choose love or to choose hate. We choose love." Take care. Best Regards, Maurice J. Blair

Tackling Several Pressing Criminal Justice and Geopolitical Issues on Labor Day 2024

CHAPTER EIGHT

<u>11:21 screenview of an 8:59 FB Messenger message</u>

This is a view of a how I followed up the earlier response with a bonus response before he made visible follow-up in the thread. - M.J.B.

8:59 PM

A few minutes ago, I went ahead and distanced myself from the hijacked account on Facebook that you used to use as your account. That was because I decided that the mojo would probably be better for everyone if I would do that. I unfriended that other Justin Haynes account-- the one you have made clear repeatedly that you have believed yourself to have no hope (or virtually no hope) of recovering control over. I had thought about doing that before several times, yet I had been repeatedly hesitant about doing that until just now, a few minutes before sending you this as a way of informing you about what went on with that. Yes, Justin Haynes with the real running of a Justin Haynes account involving you, take care. Regards, Maurice

   11:21 PM
9/8/2024

Justin's response at approximately 9 P.M. (time not stamped by FB Mssgr b/c almost immediately after M.J.B.'s 8:59 P.M. mssg)

Emirsah Mitchell
Facebook

CHAPTER EIGHT 107

A view of the beginning of M.J.B.'s 10:57 response to J.H.'s approx. 9:00 video-link seemingly-non-sequitur message:

10:57 PM

Interesting video. That being said, it is rather weird for you to try to label Liza Darnton, "some rich bitch" and "a stranger." No. In the long run she was more accepting of me in several ways than any of the other women I had ever gotten anywhere with. Of all the women I ever interacted with in any very major amount of at least a minimum amoujnt of something seemingly magical about the interaction and enough quantitiy of interaction to be something fit for evaluating, she managed the situation within a range of perfection. Others had the chance to manage their situations in interacting with me such as to have some similar arrival into a range of perfection (as deemed by my energy system of heart and mind and soul, etc.), yet all the other ones in one way or another failed during at least one or two major junctures along the way without ever fully recovering the situation for that. Yes, some guys have ended up having many women interact in ways that achieved some type of what they considered perfection, but perhaps my long-term restrictions have been a factor, and, of course, there have been so many other factors. Reiterating discussion of part of those erotic restrictions, remember how it is that since the Arthur Andersen exit interview in which they criticized my interpersonal skills in general together with other factors led to my energy system working on a largely antiejacularoty basis--except for wet dreams being considered blameless, unless and until something were to change. (For example, such as if a marriage were to seem right for bringing back for me to deem some cases of ejaculation while having sex with the wife to qualify as blameless ejaculations--that together with how the rest of the factors work are such that the vast majority of the rare occasions when I get to the level of experiencing foreplay or even sex with romantic partners (even if expanded to include if any ghosts and/or spirits--with sleep and/or some transcendental way of interacting--would supplement regular-reality observable ones) in the time since after that transition of April 19, 2001 tends to be much less of a thrill than Liza's unorthodox mouth-to-mouth kissing method was for me. Over and over again, the rare cases of erotic interaction involve my intentionally avoiding ejaculation, because my energy system has that set up that in some versions of Tantric Buddhism and some versions of Christianity this allows me to be sexually blameless while a single guy, by choosing this extreme restriction. Therefore, when people get into conflicts with me, one of the problems that they often have is that they probably assume me to not have the discipline, focus, clarity, etc. that comes from this behavioral sacrifice and everything that emanates from it. Many of them probably assume me to be blamable for many ranges of sexual activity for which I am consistently blameless, and I am willing to act on behalf of REALITY to destroy them if necessary when the conflicts escalate. We all can choose some sort of energy contract with REALITY and find out how well we live up to that energy contract, and this is very much part and parcel of that, though I acknowledge that different ways of life are best for different people in many ways, and I respect how there can and probably should be a diversity of people's energy contracts with REALITY in terms of how they regulate biological processes, including collaborative biological processes. That can be metaphorical or literal, depending on how things go. Also, if we simply let it be that there is also a degree of equivalency of first stage genuineness of interaction in some ways and that there is the long-term effect with when a given physical intimacy of kissing, footsie, foreplay, fondling, dirty dancing, sex, and similar stuff happens and things are going well, then there is the factor of whether both people feel favorable toward some type of networking or other public or semipublic acknowledgement of a carryover effect of the aftermath. At that level, it is both 1) a harsh criticism of my entire family, including me, that almost every romantic partner with whom I ever get anywhere sooner or later decides (preemptively by refusal to social network at what seems to me the right time and the right way in terms of energy system, or an alternative that would serve similarly, such as just a perfect way of how some email correspondence or something similar might go) on a need to minimize almost anything that would take the appearance of people suspecting that what happened had happened and 2) a criticism of all the women involved with at least reaching any gven base (in terms of baseball metaphor) or something similar other than Liza that those other women would each one after another at the key juncture of whether or not the second stage would happen simply reject it after I would open the door to it. There is also a degree of praise available to me for holding the line with such resolution in terms of restrictions and transformations, which set up the possibility that someone could come along and fit the situation perfectly like this,very much outside of the vast majority of how guys manage their energy contracts with REALITY such as to set up which romantic partners might effect their energy systems perfectly or not. Some of this can parallel stuff like aerobic bacteria versus anaerobic bacteria. With most people, it is forbidden most of the time to openly discuss these things in polite conversation and polite conversation, yet we've discussed it many times and maybe adding this time might help you to get to understand it better. I cooperate with that guideline from some Buddhists, some Catholics, some Protestants, and some people of other arrangements, going completely against the vast majority of the mainstream of how guys manage sexuality. BTW, and I think I mentioned it to you before, Rose Rodriguez had told me on one occasion, long after she had gotten to know me reasonably well, that she thought that my managing things in a very different way from an extremely high percentage of guys in this respect might make it more difficult to get a long-term, steady girlfriend. She did not say out loud the rationale underneath her statement of it, and I did not ask her to clarify why she thought that, yet it seemed abundantly clear to me that her idea consisted of: 1) that most gals find it part of the game to work with how most guys want very badly to experience ejaculation, especially while having sex with a desired female partner, 2) my having become the truth incarnate of fulfilling the extinction of that, in accordance with some religious guidelines by some religous people and through my own experimentations with life resulting in a conclusion that experience proves it to work very well for ,me,

unless and until something major were to change in relationship with my situation (for example, including the possibility of perhaps bringing some of it back after marriage someday if there ever is a marriage someday, or if something else very cataclysmic were to cause the kind of change to the energy contract with REALITY), and 3) therefore, although there can be paths forward for LTR for me with the right match or the right matches, my choosing to be among the extremely rare guys with such a restriction together with the disadvantages of frequently wearing glasses, having reached a stage of life of having major baldness, and other things about my appearance from the chin up, it makes the entire dynamic more difficult for a given woman to be both willing and able to navigate. Of course, as we discussed before, had my parents not been so hell-bent on stopping Rose and me from getting into some committed LTR, then maybe she and I might have had a great chance at a great marriage. However, that is water under the bridge now. Also, there are several extra things I could state here, but of course, a different angle on much of this was already expressed in some of my books, and I have already described much of it to you in person and over the phone. Another way to look at much of this is that if we do a gender-reversal of people with the Trisha Yearwood and Don Henley main studio recording of the song "Walkaway Joe," and we draw a parallel, what we get is that it is easy that if a woman has at least one major ulterior motive or at least one major character flaw or both in her interaction with me in the short run, it could be overcome if she grows out of those flaws enough in the medium run or the long run, much as I have grown out of many flaws over time, such that then she and I could in the long run both feel fine about a degree of what an earlier part of this message labeled the second stage. However, when a woman is (as compared and contrasted with some spiritual transcendence) driven excessively by 1) concern for her status with her girlfriends, 2) concern for whether some people from some cool crowd might start to imagine her to not be cool enough, 3) worried about people from society in general thinking that she once had low standards in terms of their way of judging her (for example, although Jessica Trend was in some ways perfect in her interactions with me, in other ways she was nowhere near perfect with them, because she found the police officer tapping the window with the flashlight and the other patterns to be such that she decided upon wanting nothing to do with ever planning any more dating or any other face-to-face meetings with me, and would not even choose to confirm for me that her surname of the pronunciation of "Trend" was actually spelled like it sounded; although in almost any regular sense I made it much further with her than I did with Liza, the complete pattern does not earn for her anywhere near the ethereal level of perfection that Liza achieved), 4) thinking that there is something embarassing that should be swept under a rug (sometimes overlapping with #3, other times different), 5) thinking that if she can interact in a way that feeds her with legal residency status and/or money as an advantage while not really feeling thoroughly genuine

CHAPTER EIGHT

benevolence and interest, or 6) whatever else, it tends to be easy for her to eventually focus on whatever she finds incompatible with that, then to avoid even a minimum amount of a gateway for the public to notice some evidence of a legacy. Liza was both the first to choose a very genuine romantic personal display of affection toward me, and, over 27 years later, she became the first of those to choose something--to whatever degree inspired by enlightened motives or anything else--a clear step of agreeing with me on something that would from my experience of reality fit the situation as a fulfilment of that second stage. Jessica had the chance and chose against it. Rose had the chance and chose against it. Similarly with several others. At some core level of the spiritual resonance, the ones other than Liza at some stage at a crossroads of becoming like the guy in "Walkaway Joe" who walks away wind up achieving something first stage magical (inclusion of physical magic, to one degree or another) with me, then when there is a chance for them to collaborate with me on second stage (augmenting the legacy of the physical magic with something that rings true as holistic magic), they would one after another bascially fall flat on their faces in terms of what it meant to me. Of course, maybe all of them or maybe most of them might have been right to do that, because the combination of their not achieving that second stage in collaboration with me, and Liza's achievement of the second stage in collaboration with me is enough that there is a core level at which Liza Darnton has had, even in the absence of becoming a family member of mine and even in the absence of having become a friend in any regular sense of mine, and even in the absence of having become a big-time religious, political, or business leader, and even in the absenc of having become a medical doctor of mine, yes, even in all those absences, she has holistically proven more healing toward me than anyone else. For people who might have read *Alternative Beginnings and Endings of All Things: Science, Religion, Politics, and Cards, Hypervolume II* thoroughly, it could eventually arrive that they could perhaps feel and know much of this without having to be told all of it. Indeed, much of what I am telling you here is a rephrasing and a repetition of some of what I mentioned there, yet some of what I have described here is also somewhat beyond the expressions there. On another note, in terms of cold hard cash of financial accounts, my draft will is not on track to leave very much to much of anyone other than my next of kin. Yes, some intellectual property is on track to be divided such as to have a significant amount of it go to my next of kin, but this is nowhere nearly as high a percentage going to next of kin in the case of those copyrights and related stuff. In contrast, with the financial accounts, my next of kin are sitting at--before expenses--over 90% on the parts that wind up not already having "payable on death" or "transferrable on death" set up. Part of that, also, is to try to make sure that my next of kin have a good chance of getting something substantial left after lawyers, possible professional executors, and any other expenses/fees. Also, if I get married, then my next of kin will probably have total or nearly-total control on the accounts that have POD/TOD settings. Now, there are other twists and turns to this entire discussion that I could go into right now, but they would probably be better for me to save for presentation another time and in another way.

Sent 35m ago

Thus concluded my 10:57 P.M. U.S. CDT message that concluded the 8 SEP 2024 part of that debate. - M. James Blair

  11:33 PM 9/8/2024

CHAPTER EIGHT

In the morning after the fiery September 8, 2024 debate via one-to-one Facebook Messenger direct messages, I decided to do one more direct one-to-one message to tie up a loose end and to segue into creating a group message

7:28 AM

Another thing, Justin, is that, in many respects, I refuted your recent opening attack of a remark--refuted for those who could competently read and comprehend what I stated--although I did not directly address head on that very statement you had toward me of, "You're an idiot." There are several peculiar features with the words and concepts of labeling people as "idiots," "fools," "sages," "wisemen," "wisewomen," "good people," "bad people," and "mediocre people." If anyone is hell-bent on condemning anyone else, then the contemner can at least temporarily think of anyone who has ever lived as having been an idiot, a fool, or both, yet that does not make such a contemner necessarily correct for doing so. The next message, in which I shall place you and at least one other person on the same Facebook message, shall delve deeper into this issue. Cheers! M.J.B.

Sent

  7:29 AM
9/9/2024

Outline of people included in a message to multiple people in the morning of 9 SEP 2024:

Members

Facebook profile photos redacted from this display for the purposes of presenting this copy of a direct electronic text from M.J.B. to J.H., A.M., C.Q., J.D., R.T., and W.W.

All   Admins

Alex Pacheco
Added by you

Armando Martinez
Added by you

Carisa Quintana
Added by you

Jennifer Dai
Added by you

Justin Haynes
Added by you

Maurice James Blair
Group creator

Radically Transformed
Added by you

William Woo
Added by you

FACEBOOK PROFILE PHOTOS REDACTED FOR THIS MESSAGE COPY'S PRESENTATION.

10:10 AM

A FEW ORIENTATIONS IN PREPARATION FOR UNDERSTANDING THE MAIN, ORIGINAL CHOICE OF AUDIENCE FOR THE GROUP FACEBOOK MESSENGER MESSAGE THAT FOLLOWED UP ON THE ONE-TO-ONE DIRECT MESSAGING DEBATE BETWEEN JUSTIN AND ME:

Alex Pacheco and I were high school classmates way back when.

Armando Martinez and I met in elementary school.

Carisa Quintana and I met via the University of Texas at Austin, McCombs School of Business, Master in Professional Accounting program that she and I both attended and completed from Fall Semester 2000 to Spring Semester 2002. Her surname was different back then, and I am choosing that it should be treated as on a need-to-know basis. Thus I decline to state here what her maiden name was.

Jennifer Dai and I met in portions of the 1980s and 1990s via a church that was Grant Avenue Baptist Church and later changed its name to El Paso Chinese Baptist Church.

William Woo and I also met via that church; he eventually found his way into serving in the clergy of another location of a church.

Screenshot 2 of viewing a message sent to multiple people early on 9 SEP 2024:

You created this group

Add   Name

9:59 AM

Greetings Recipients, Here for your consideration is something adjacent to much of the past interaction that has happened anywhere between anyone and anyone else, and which is also core to much of how things might proceed from here. Recently, one of you, specifically the one with a Facebook display name Justin Haynes, brought up {via his making an accusation of idiocy (within a direct, one-to-one message to me via Facebook messenger, and to which I responded with a series of direct, one-to-one messaging to him)} the issue of when, how, and why anyone ever accuses anyone else of idiocy. Consider

   10:12 AM 9/9/2024

CHAPTER EIGHT

Screenshot 3 of a 09:59 A.M. U.S. CDT 9 SEP 2024 message

how there could be no position that anyone anywhere could have such as to avoid the possibility of an accusation of wrong-mindedness--even in some cases to the point of an outright accusation of idiocy--if fully threatened by at least one group fitting the profile of at least one of the following: 1) How Christopher Hitchens expressed condemnation of the core logic of Christianity itself in a portion of audiovisual footage titled on YouTube as, "The Immoral Teachings of Christianity," 2) People who conceptualize any of "the true interpretations of Christianity" to "have to be" what they could call, "The Moral Teachings of Christianity," 3) People who would truly believe in one specific Abrahamic religion, one sect thereof, one subsect thereof, and/or a cult thereof amounting to identifying as clearly "other than Christianity" and as "alleging complete claim" to "the truth" while conceiving Reality to demand for people to avoid identifying as Christians, 4) People who do not affiliate primarily with any of the

10:25 AM
9/9/2024

(Here is screenshot 4 (of 11) of a 9:59 A.M. September 9, 2024 Facebook message.)

first three in this list, yet who believe that everyone should closely replicate some straightforward way of religiously aligning with themselves at some basic level of logic, and 5) People of any specific political persuasion who believe that anyone who identifies with some specific competing political persuasion definitely being idiots. Of course, #5 on that list is sufficient all by itself in some countries sometimes to render there to be no place within any range of beliefs to be able to escape from having at least some people accuse idiocy. Likewise, when one person expresses a belief to another person that the second person has no right to value a third person as highly as the second person values the third person, and the first person hardly understands much of the genuineness and truth of what had happened under the surface in terms of the interaction, then that first person could be very much off base to hurl the accusation of idiocy.

10:27 AM
9/9/2024

CHAPTER EIGHT

SCREENSHOT 5 (of 11) OF A MESSAGE:

> Yet, flip the script for a little while, and recognize that within the way of hurling approval toward people, even to the level of calling someone a sage, a wiseman, a wisewoman, or a great leader, etc: that is also something that people can at times jump into way too much of, something they can take way too far. Also, at a time when Bob Dylan found his entire life's situation terrible in many respects, he hurled a degree of an accusation of idiocy toward almost everyone he knew or knew of, including himself, via the song "Idiot Wind." Shifting gears now. A book titled *San Min Chu I: The Three Principles of the People* by Sun Yat-sen and translated into English by Frank W. Price (a copy of which I have consulted portions of in a few recent years; note that the copy indicates "Published by China Cultural Service 1985" / "Taipei, Taiwan, Republic of China" and yet does not seem to display any ISBN for itself on that copy) includes at least a passage or two expressing a way of contrasts along a
>
> 10:29 AM
> 9/9/2024

Screenshot 6 of a 09:59 Hours on 09 SEP 2024 message

range of people exhibiting the least amounts of mental competence (i.e., those whom it refers to as "the mentally ill") to people exhibiting the greatest amounts of mental competence (i.e., those whom it refers to as "the sages"). Of course, that book also discusses a great many other ideas on controversial subjects, yet that serves as an example of how people can think long and hard about whom to consider as sages versus whom to consider as falling a little short of being sages versus whom to consider as falling way below the level of being sages, etc. Another set of things to consider could be how both Benjamin Franklin and Shabkar Tsokdruk Rangdrol expressed long ago that REALITY could very much transcend some extreme either-or type of logic of adherence to idea structures. Later, scientists found something that profoundly illustrates much of this issue, namely that experimental tests have shown a consistency of our physically-observable reality of lightwaves and such refuting

10:30 AM
9/9/2024

CHAPTER EIGHT

Screenshot 7 (of 11) of a September 9, 2024 message

the absoluteness of what many presume to be "the common sense idea of relative motion." Although many can think of it as common sense that with steady rates of movement, "you go at constant speed w in a direction" combined with "someone else goes at constant speed v in that same direction relative to you" has to add up to "w+v" compared to the ground (or whatever fixed comparison item), replacing it with a more nuanced answer. That more nuanced answer that has experimentally consistently demonstrated itself to be real in terms of normal physics is as follows: It approximates to the common sense "w+v" at speeds that are slow compared to the speed of light, yet it more technically conforms in those conditions to "(w+v)/(1+(wv)/c^2)." In other words, the vast majority of human beings nowadays might go around believing reality to conform to their "common sense idea" that velocities always add up in a simple-minded "1+1=2" kind of way, whereas ACTUALLY-EXPERIMENTALLY-TESTED-REPEATEDLY-ON-MANY-PAST-OCCASIONS REALITY has consistently conformed to that adding up as "1+1=extremely close to 2"

10:31 AM
9/9/2024

under many conditions--specifically slow compared to lightspeed--of day-to-day stuff, but if the velocities are close to the speed of light, with '1' (unit in context) being a high percentage of the speed of light (traveling at a constant velocity compared to an inertial reference frame), then it could be barely above 1. In that case "1+1=something that can be barely larger than 1." (Also, the classic extreme of that is that if w=c and v=c, then we see that the speed of light going forward within a vehicle can be measured by someone in the vehicle as going at c even though someone outside the vehicle can also measure it as traveling at c, even if the vehicle is going at 99% of c. Therefore, some people would think, "0.99c+c=1.99c," whereas reality could be ready to slap them with, "Whether on board the vehicle going at 0.99c compared to the ground, the light moving forward within the vehicle is still traveling at c.") When people go through life with some of their ideas ironed through their minds through and through and think of their thoughts and the thoughts of others as having to

10:33 AM
9/9/2024

> **Screenshot 9 of a 09:59 Hrs CDT, Sep. 9, 2024 message**
>
> always be that way, then coalescing into groups to slam that down on others, it can be like: A says to B, "I am of this set of thoughts, and you are of that set of thoughts; I am absolutely, unequivocally right, and you are absolutely and unequivocally wrong. B says to A, "No. I am of this other set of thoughts, and you are of the set of thoughts that you choose, and I am absolutely, unequivocally right, and you are absolutely and unequivocally wrong." Then they go back and forth ad infinitem. In that case, often, each set of them may be missing that Modern Physics already undercut the absoluteness of many overly-simple-mindedly-logical ideas of reality over a century ago. That boat has sailed. That being said, there are portions of scripture within each of the ancient major religions that already pointed toward how that boat would eventually sail in modern times as it did. Buddhism--from a perspective tending to emphasize austerity--and Taoism--from a perspective tending to emphasize subtlety--went through that over and over again in many of their main statements from thousands of years ago.

Note the missing apostrophe and the oddity of showing "ad infinitem" in place of the standard "ad infinitum." The endnotes include a reiteration that adjusts for those and a few other issues.[4]

SCREENSHOT 10 (of 11) OF A MESSAGE:

> Christianity in at least a few spots has escape clauses that go straight into it also (e.g., *John* 9:39--with the symbolism of the value both of losing fixed vision and of losing fixed absence of vision, thereby acquiring new liberty from past vision and new liberty of acquiring new vision) can function in the minds of those who use it that way as a full way of accessing the same sort of thing that Buddhism, Taoism, and Modern Physics tend to express of transcending a simple-minded absolute and excessive adherence to limited cognition of very limited idea structure patterns.) Consider again any one of the three sides of the Jefferson, Hitchens, and Lewis dynamic of which Hitchens expressed a strong adherence to one side in that video mentioned earlier, and which is available at the Youtube location that after the Youtube.com/ part of it has watch?v=D7UImBPq4WI. Contrast it with things of your choice. Next, here is another set.

CHAPTER EIGHT

> Although Olivia Newton-John expressed that she did not get into any very thorough studies of the physics that her maternal grandfather--a fellow named Max Born--had helped to revolutionize, she did express a song that could be controversial for some people yet intuitively sensible to other people with "The Way of Love" (a manifestation of which is available at the Youtube location that after the Youtube.com/ part of it has watch?v=ehwrEjuY3Yk). If people compare and contrast that song with *Deuteronomy*, Chapter 13, the process could help to illustrate how *John* 9:39 can be considered to point toward something that could be thought of as akin to how Lee in *Enter the Dragon* expressed the idea that beings should take care not to excessively focus on "a finger pointing toward the moon" such as to be distracted from "the moon" itself, as paralleling to refrain from having ideas regarding REALITY distract from more directly recognizing and experiencing REALITY ITSELF. Regards, M.J. Blair

Screenshot 11 (of 11) of a 9:59 CDT, 9 SEP 2024 Facebook message from M.J.B. to multiple recipients

Endnotes:

1. **An elderly man mentioned that in Las Vegas on July 31, 2022, and he identified himself as Floyd Brotherson, a military veteran who had served for the United States of America.** Among the people who heard him state that was me, Maurice James Blair, the author of this book. What happens in Vegas may usually stay in Vegas, but sometimes what happens in Vegas escapes, paralleling quantum tunneling.

2. Cf. **https://fiscaldata.treasury.gov/datasets/debt-to-the-penny/debt-to-the-penny** as accessed Sep. 1, 2024.

3. **"In the beginning, Reality began."**
   Some would strongly agree with that statement.

   "In the beginning, Reality continued."
Others would agree with that contrasting statement.

   • Consider whatever overlap, if any, there could be in those who might transcend mundane conceptualization to agree with both statements.

   • Also consider possibilities of mind involving simultaneously letting go of both statements, and thereby transcending: to lack attachment to the one and lack attachment to the other.

Many have estimated the Earth to be incredibly old in terms of the historico-scientific realm.
   Imagine witnessing it as The Beginning of the World Known as Earth Happens.

4. A restatement of one of the passages from a September 9, 2024 message while utilizing a few adjustments to it:

When people go through life with some of their ideas ironed through their minds through and through and think of their thoughts and the thoughts of others as having to always be that way, then coalescing into groups to slam that down on others, it can be like:

> A says to B, "I am of this set of thoughts, and you are of that set of thoughts; I am absolutely, unequivocally right, and you are absolutely and unequivocally wrong."

> B says to A, "No. I am of this other set of thoughts, and you are of the set of thoughts that you choose, and I am absolutely, unequivocally right, and you are absolutely and unequivocally wrong."

Then they go back and forth ad infinitum.

Although some can conduct debates in that style while beneath the surface being fully cognizant of transcendence, it can often be the case, rather, that each at some levels of mind clings to an obliviousness to how Modern

Physics already undercut the absoluteness of many overly-simple-mindedly-logical ideas of reality over a century ago.

That boat has sailed.

Having stated that, though, bear in mind that there are portions of ancient religions that had already pointed outward very long in advance toward how that boat would eventually sail in modern times as it did.

EPILOGUE: A PROJECTION FOR THE PERIOD FROM DECEMBER 31, 2024 TO A WHILE ONWARD

December 31, 2024: Revelers in many locations celebrate New Year's Eve.

January 1, 2025: Revelers in many time zones celebrate New Year's Day 2025.

* * * * * * * * * * *

Flashforward now to what many scientists, many theologians, and many everyday people believe will eventually happen:
    Whether caused by the Sun expanding such as to consume the Earth, a supermassive explosion, An Extraordinary Being making All Regular Reality go away, or by anyone or anything else, The End of The World Known as Earth Happens, and—in at least some sense—Reality Goes On.

THE END.

www.ingramcontent.com/pod-product-compliance
Lightning Source LLC
Chambersburg PA
CBHW041455010526
44107CB00014B/1045